D1595861

Middle
Beyond
Extremes

Middle
Beyond
Extremes

Maitreya's *Madhyāntavibhāga*
with commentaries by
Khenpo Shenga and Ju Mipham

Translated by
The Dharmachakra Translation
Committee

Snow Lion Publications
Ithaca, New York
Boulder, Colorado

Snow Lion Publications
P.O. Box 6483
Ithaca, New York 14851 USA
(607) 273-8519
www.snowlionpub.com

Cover photograph and design by Rafael Ortet

Illustrations:
Asaṅga (p. 7), by Gomchen Oleshe
Representation of Mipham's outline (p.166), courtesy of Tsadra Foundation

Printed in the USA on acid-free recycled paper

ISBN-13: 978-1-55939-270-9
ISBN-10: 1-55939-270-3

Library of Congress Cataloging-in-Publication Data

Mi-pham-rgya-mtsho, 'Jam-mgon 'Ju, 1846-1912.
   [Dbus mtha' rnam 'byed kyi 'grel pa 'od zer phreṅ ba. English]
   Middle beyond extremes: Maitreya's Madhyantavibhanga with commentaries / by
Khenpo Shenga and Ju Mipham; translated by Dharmachakra Translation Committee.
   p. cm.
   Maitreyanātha's work translated into English from the Tibetan translation of the original
Sanskrit text.
   Includes bibliographical references and index.
   ISBN-13: 978-1-55939-270-9 (alk. paper)
   ISBN-10: 1-55939-270-3 (alk. paper)
   1. Maitreyanātha. Madhyāntavibhaṅga. 2. Yogācāra (Buddhism) I. Maitreyanātha.
Madhyāntavibhaṅga. English. II. Gźan-phan-chos-kyi-snaṅ-ba, Gźan-dga', 1871-1927.
Dbus daṅ mtha' rnam par 'byed pa'i mchan 'grel. English. III. Title.
   BQ2967.M55813 2007
   294.3'420423--dc22

                                                                2006024698

TABLE OF CONTENTS

Asaṅga

Thupten Choeling Monastery
Junbesi, No. 3, Eastern Nepal

P.O. Box 2834
Kathmandu, Nepal
Tel : 479045

FOREWORD

by Trulshik Rinpoche

Our compassionate teacher, the fourth guide of this Excellent Eon, speaks of "the well-spoken words and the commentaries." With this, he refers to the innumerable sūtras and tantras, as well as all the treatises that illumine their enlightened intent. The Regent Maitreyanātha, lord of the ten grounds, granted five treatises to the master Asaṅga in the divine realm of Tuṣita, two of which are concerned with "distinguishing." This book contains an English translation of one of these two treatises, namely *Distinguishing the Middle from Extremes*.

Accompanying Maitreya's teaching are two commentaries: The first, composed by Khenchen Shenga, was created by means of a classic Indian source. The book also contains the explanations by Mipham Nampar Gyalwa, our loving protector and king of Dharma. In this way, it contains, as it were, both Indian and Tibetan commentaries.

Under the auspices of the Dharmachakra Translation Committee, these texts have been translated by students of the supreme refuge, Chökyi Nyima Rinpoche. Headed by Thomas Doctor, who is devoted, committed, and knowledgeable, the translators attended lectures on the texts by learned scholars, and endeavoring to clarify their understanding, they diligently brought forth these English versions. Rejoicing in this, I wish to express my congratulations and thanks. I supplicate, pray, and invoke the truth of the Three Jewels, that whoever studies and reflects on these texts may experience the glorious two-fold accomplishment.

This was written by Trulshik of Dzarong, who is in all regards deluded, but bears the title of Khenpo, on the 15th day of the 3rd month in the fire dog year, the year 2133 of the Tibetan kings (2006).

Chökyi Nyima Rinpoche, President

Dharmachakra Translation Committee
P.O. Box 21277, Boudhanath, Kathmandu, Nepal
www.dharmachakra.net

༄༅། །མཐའ་ཡས་པའི་སེམས་ཅན་ཡོངས་ཀྱི་མ་འདྲེས་པའི་མཛོད་བཞེས་ཆེན་པོ་སྟོན་པ་ཡང་དག་པར་ཕྱོགས་
པའི་སངས་རྒྱས་བཅོམ་ལྡན་འདས་ཀྱི་བཀའ་མོ་ལུགས་རྒྱུད་ལུང་མན་ངག་དང་། དེའི་དགོངས་འགྲེལ་
མདོ་ལུགས་བསྟན་བཅོས་རིག་གནས་དང་བཅས་པ་ཁྱབ་ཆེར་བོད་གངས་ཅན་པའི་སྐད་དུ་སྒྱུར་སྟོབ་ཆོས་
གསུམ་དང་། རྒྱ་བོད་ཀྱི་པ་བྱང་ལ་མ་རྗེས་འབྲངས་དང་བཅས་པས་འཆད་ཉན་པ་བསྒྱུར་སྒྲུབ་ཉམས་
ལེན་ཚད་ལྡན་བྱས་པའི་བཀའ་དྲིན་གྱི་འདས་ཡུར་མཁས་ཤིང་གྲུབ་པའི་གོ་འཕང་མཐོ་པོར་གཤེགས་པ་
མཁས་གྲུབ་གནས་མེད་དཔར་སྟོན་ལ། དེ་རྣམས་ཀྱི་རྒྱལ་བའི་བཀའ་དང་དེའི་དགོངས་འགྲེལ་བསྒྱུར་
བཅོས་རིག་གནས་དང་བཅས་པར་ཡང་འགྱེལ་དང་། གཞན་ཡང་མཁས་གྲུབ་དག་པ་དེ་དག་གི་གསུང་
འབུམ་སོགས་པོད་གང་ང་སྟོང་ཕྱག་མང་ཡོད་པའི་པོད་གངས་ཅན་པའི་གཞི་རྟེན་ཉོན་ཁྱད་འཕགས་གཅིག་དུ་
ལྷུ་དུ་ཡིན་ཅིང་། དེང་སྐབས་འཛིན་སྐྱིང་པའི་མི་སྐུ་སྐུ་ཚོགས་ཀྱིས་དེ་དག་ལ་དོ་སྣང་དང་དད་གུས་བཙུགས་
འགྱུས་ཆེན་པོས་ཐོས་བསམ་སྒོམ་སྒྲུབ་མཛོད་མཁན་ཉི་མར་དུ་འགྲོ་བཞིན་པ་འདི་ནི་དམ་པའི་ཆོས་ཀྱི་ཡོན་ཏན་
དང་། དགོས་པ་རྒྱ་མཚོན་ཆེ་གསལ་མཆིན་པ་ལ་བརྟེན་ནས་ཡུང་གོར་མ་ཆགས་ཤེང་། དེར་བརྟེན་ད་ལམ་
ས་བརྟུབེ་དབང་ཕྱུག་རྒྱལ་ཚོ་བྲམས་ས་མགོན་པོའི་གསུང་ཐེག་པ་ཆེན་པོའི་གཞུང་བྲམས་ཚོས་སྟེ་ལྟ་ནི་ཐེག་
ཆེན་ལྟ་སྒོམ་སྤྱོད་འབྲས་དང་བཅས་པ་ཆོས་ལ་མ་ནོར་བ་བཞིན་ཏུ་ཟབ་ཅིང་བཙིད་ལ་རྒྱ་ཆེ་བ་ལུང་རིགས་མན་
དག་གི་ལྷུག་པ་ཡིན་ལ། སྐྱེ་སྒྲིའི་ལ་གྲུས་དབུས་མཐའ་རྣམ་འབྱེད་ཀྱི་འགྲེལ་པ་མཁས་ཆེ་གཞན་དགས་རྒྱ་
གཞུང་ལས་བཏུས་པ་དེ་དང་། མཁས་མཆོག་ཚི་མི་ཕམ་ཕྱོགས་ལས་རྣམ་པར་རྒྱལ་བའི་འཕྱེལ་ལ་བཅས་པ།
ཏོས་ཀྱི་སྒྲོ་ཕྱུག་དང་བཙུགིན་ཤེས་རབ་ཅན། ཧོ་མ་སེ་ཌ་ག་ཏར། གཙོས་ཚོས་འཛིན་སྐྱ་སྒྱུར་ཚོགས་མིས་
མཁས་པ་ཁག་ནས་དཔེ་ཕྱིད་དང་། དོ་གས་གཙོད་བཅས་འབད་པ་ཆེ་པོས་དཔྱི་སྐད་དུ་ཕབ་བསྒྱུར་བྱས་
པར་སྐྱིད་ནས་དགའ་མགུ་ཡི་རངས་ཀྱི་སྒོ་ནས་བསྔགས་བརྗོད་ཀྱི་མེ་ཏོག་ཡང་ཡང་འཐོར་རྒྱུ་དང་། རྒྱ་ཆེ་
གཉིགས་པོ་རྣམས་ནས་རབ་ད་དཔེ་བྱིད་ལུ་རྒྱུ་དང་། ཡང་ན་དོ་གས་གཙོས་མཛོད་གལ་ཆེ་ལ་ལ་གཞུང་འདི་
དག་རྒྱགས་ཆུམས་སུ་བསྒྱུར་ན་རིང་པོར་མི་ཐོག་པར་རང་ཉིད་བྱང་ཆུབ་ཆེན་པོའི་གོ་འཕང་བརྗེས་ཤེང་པར་
ཕྱིན་དྲུག་གསོགས་པའི་སྒོ་ནས་མཐའ་ཡས་འགྲོ་བ་འདི་བའི་དོན་དགའོ་ཆེན་པོ་འབྱུར་བར་གདོན་མི་ཟ་ར་
རང་གཞན་ཀུན་གྱི་འཆང་ཉན་དང་། ཉམས་ལེན་ཚུལ་བཞིན་གནང་གས་ཆ་ལགས་ན་དེ་བཞིན་ཕུགས་
དུས་སུ་བསྐི་བར་གསོལ་ལ་འདེབས་པ་པོ་ཆོས་ཀྱི་ཉི་མ་སྤྲུལ་མིང་པས་བོད་རྒྱལ་ལོ་ ༢༡༣༣ རབ་བྱུང་
༡༣ ཤིང་བྱ་ཟླ་ ༡༡ ཚོས་ ༡༥ དང་། སྤྱི་ལོ་ ༢༠༠༧ ཟླ་ ༡ ཚོས་ ༡༠ ཉིན་བྲིས།།

FOREWORD

by Chökyi Nyima Rinpoche

Our teacher, the truly and completely Awakened One, the Transcendent Conqueror, is the great, implicit friend of all sentient beings, limitless in number. The teachings he gave can be divided into sūtra and mantra, and further into tantra, scripture, and instruction. The essential meaning of these, in turn, is explained in the classic treatises of the sūtra and mantra traditions. Along with those related to the mundane fields of learning, the majority of these literary works were translated into Tibetan, the language of the Land of Snows.

The preceptor Śāntarakṣita, the master Padmasambhava, and the Dharma King Trisong Deutsen, as well as the many learned and accomplished masters of India and Tibet and those who became their followers, all pursued study, teaching, translation, and the practice of meditation in a perfect manner. As a result of their altruistic works, the number of individuals who reached truly high levels of scholarly expertise and spiritual accomplishment became so large that today they cannot be counted.

The literary output of these masters includes commentaries and subcommentaries that explain the Buddha's teachings, the classic treatises, and the mundane fields of learning. It is a literature that contains vast collections of masterful, original writings. These many thousands of volumes constitute, as it were, the one extraordinary, true treasure of Tibet, the Land of Snows. Currently this great body of literature is attracting increasing attention from many sides, and a growing number of people from all over the world engage in study, reflection, and meditation with great enthusiasm and devotion. This is undoubtedly due to an increasingly clear perception of the sacred Dharma's quality, purpose, and scope.

In his Five Teachings the protector Maitreya, the Regent who has mastered the ten grounds, reveals fully and flawlessly the view, meditation, conduct and fruition that is accomplished through the Great Vehicle. With utmost profundity his teachings reach far and wide; they are a treasury of scripture, reasoning, and oral instruction.

This book contains one among his five treatises, *Distinguishing the Middle from Extremes*. It is accompanied by two commentaries: Khenchen Shenga's elucidations, which are all drawn from a classical Indian source, and the explanations of the supreme scholar, Mipham Chokley Nampar Gyalwa. These English translations were prepared under the auspices of the Dharmachakra Translation Committee. They were produced by a group of translators headed by my student, Thomas Doctor, who is devoted, committed, and knowledgeable. The translators followed a series of lectures on the texts, and they have worked hard to clarify their understanding with the help of several scholars. I wholeheartedly delight and rejoice in their efforts and repeatedly toss flowers of praise.

To those who read this book I would recommend following a program of lectures, since this is the best way to meet these texts. In any case, it is important that one actively seek to gain a clear understanding of these teachings. Whoever practices them will, without a doubt, before long accomplish the stage of great enlightenment and, by relying on factors such as the six transcendences, arise as a great captain to guide all wandering beings. It is therefore important for us all to study and correctly practice these teachings, and so I humbly request that these issues be taken to heart.

This was written by Chökyi Nyima, who has been given the name of Tulku, on the 15th day of the 11th month in the wood bird year of the 17th cycle, the year 2132 of the Tibetan kings (14th of January, 2006).

INTRODUCTION

Twelve long years of austere practice in solitary retreat had brought the noble Asaṅga to an extraordinary level of spiritual maturity. In turning to Maitreya, Regent of the Buddha Śākyamuni and embodiment of perfect love, his heart and mind had become profoundly receptive, moistened and nourished by the waters of love. Yet while his spiritual awakening was soon to set in motion a liberating wave of events that would reach millions, Asaṅga was not aware of the deep changes that had been taking place within himself. In fact, he saw himself as a failure. His heart was as cold as ever, he thought, and the vision of the profound reality that the Buddha had discovered remained a distant and elusive dream. During his many years in retreat he had been at the verge of complete despair before, but each time some incident had occurred that would remind him both of the futility of mundane pursuits and the power of perseverance. This time, however, all hope for accomplishment had left him. Distressed by what he felt was a complete lack of progress, Asaṅga sadly decided to leave his hermitage for good.

As the dejected yogi walked the painful path back to the world of men—a world he had thought only to return to once he would be able to share with it the liberating elixir of the divine Dharma—he came across a sick and howling dog, lying by the wayside. Asaṅga stopped, and as he looked closer he saw that the dog suffered from a large open wound, infested with maggots. This pitiful sight moved Asaṅga deeply. Forgetting his depression, he knelt down by the dog and tried to think of a way that he could save it from the invading parasites without hurting the maggots or depriving them of their necessary sustenance. A solution came to his mind. Having obtained a sharp knife from a nearby village, Asaṅga resolutely cut a piece of flesh from his own thigh and placed it on the ground next to the howling and snapping dog. Intending to carefully lick off the maggots with his tongue, and then transport them safely to this fresh lump of food, he now drew his face close to the dog's oozing wound. Revolted by the sight of the maggots feasting on the rotting flesh, Asaṅga closed his eyes. But his tongue never reached the wound. Puzzled, Asaṅga opened his eyes, and at that very moment, suddenly and miraculously, he experienced the overwhelming presence of the master of infinite love. Finally, he had come face to face with radiant beauty and profound brilliance; Maitreya stood before him. "Why," Asaṅga found himself exclaiming, "have you waited so long? How could you not respond to my calls?" "I was always with you," answered the great Bodhisattva, "but it is only now that your compassion has become strong enough to sweep away the veils in your mind, which have kept my presence unknown to you." To prove his point to a still rather doubtful Asaṅga, Maitreya asked to be brought to the nearby village. Asaṅga, carrying Maitreya on his shoulders, went through the entire settlement, yet it became clear that none of the villagers could see the great Bodhisattva. Deeply moved, Asaṅga now once more repeated the supplication that had been on his lips throughout his years in retreat: "Reveal to me the definitive meaning, the profound intent of the sūtras of transcendent knowledge!"

In an instant, Asaṅga was transported to the heavenly realm of Tuṣita, and here Maitreya revealed to him the full beauty of the Supreme Vehicle, showing him the inconceivably profound and vast meanings that liberate the hearts of the Bodhisattvas and enable them to lead all beings into consummate enlightenment. When Asaṅga returned to this world he was transformed, a living treasury of the Dharma. Imbued with Maitreya's powerful teachings, he entered history as the master who established the Approach of Vast Activity, and so, comparable only to Nāgārjuna, he continues to render unimaginable service to the teachings of the Buddha and to sentient beings.

In this way the Tibetan masters Buton (bu ston, 1290-1364) and Tāranātha (born 1575) describe the emergence of Maitreya's Five Teachings (*byams chos sde lnga*)[1] in this world.[2] Upon his return from Tuṣita, Asaṅga committed some of Maitreya's teachings to writing and among them we find *Distinguishing the Middle from Extremes*. In these instructions, Maitreya describes the multifaceted, interdependent processes whereby consciousness manifests and expresses itself. He also points to the actual, intrinsic nature of these processes—a nature that, devoid of both object and subject, neither exists as process nor as consciousness. The path, he explains, is unified knowledge and compassion. Experience with this seamlessness allows us to see beyond the blinding extremes of conceptual constructs. When, on this path of experience, we equally acknowledge the expressions of mind and their intrinsic nature we will, he promises, discover a flawless and bountiful perspective—a discovery of unlimited resources.

In India the great philosopher Vasubandhu (fl. 4th century C.E.), who is reported to have been Asaṅga's younger brother, wrote a commentary to the root stanzas.[3] This commentary was further expanded on by the prolific Sthiramati,[4] who according to the same sources was Vasubandhu's direct disciple.[5] At some point during the period of the Early Translations (*snga 'gyur*) the great Yeshe De (ye shes sde, 8th century) translated *Distinguishing the Middle from Extremes*,[6] along with both of the aforementioned classical commentaries,[7] from Sanskrit into Tibetan. This book contains our humble attempt at further rendering into English Yeshe De's translation of *Distinguishing the Middle from Extremes*. We present the pithy stanzas in the company of two quite different commentaries that nevertheless are intimately related.

KHENCHEN SHENGA AND THE THIRTEEN CLASSICS

In the way that is characteristic of an "annotation-commentary" (*mchan 'grel*), Shenphen Chökyi Nangwa (gzhan phan chos kyi snang ba, 1871-1927), who is widely known as Khenpo Shenga (mkhan po gzhan dga'),[8] intersperses glosses and explanatory remarks between the words of the root text.[9] This format lets the reader begin the process of unpacking the condensed message of the verses without ever losing sight of them. Unique to Shenga's approach is that he literally never adds a word of his own. All of his comments are extracted verbatim from Vasubandhu's classical commentary.

Shenga's annotation-commentary, which appears distinguishable by indentation right after the root verses, belongs to a set of thirteen such commentaries to classical Indian texts.[10] These commentaries to the "thirteen classics" (*gzhung chen bcu gsum*) have, across traditional affiliations, become essential to the curriculum in many of the monastic colleges of Tibet, Nepal, Bhutan, and India. As an exponent of the non-sectarian Rimé (*ris med*) movement that had been initiated by Jamyang Khyentse Wangpo ('jam dbyangs mkhyen brtse'i dbang po, 1820-1892), Chokgyur Lingpa (mchog gyur gling pa, 1829-1870), and Kongtrul Lodrö Thaye

(kong sprul blo gros mtha' yas, 1813-1899), Shenga wished aspiring
Tibetan scholars to gain thorough and firsthand experience with the classics of Indian Mahāyāna Buddhism. He hoped that, with such a back-
ground, emerging scholars would be able to identify and avoid the trap
of sectarianism, which is debilitating for both society in general and the
spirit of the individual. Likewise, he and other masters of the Rimé movement felt that this type of education would be the most efficient way to
empower future generations to truly benefit from the rich and diverse
approaches that had developed during the many centuries of Buddhist
teaching and practice in Tibet. Shenga's commentaries to the Thirteen
Classics are therefore meant as a kind of "access to the source" that will
enable scholar-practitioners to genuinely appropriate and participate in
their own unique traditions, while at the same time opening their minds
to a vast range of valuable approaches.[11]

THE *GARLAND OF RADIANT LIGHT*

Shenga's commentary speaks with the authority of the ancient masters.
It is both weighty and concise, and yet it carries a tone of mystery. In
this book our attempt at translating this commentary is joined with the
Garland of Radiant Light, Ju Mipham's ('ju mi pham, 1846-1912)[12] explanations to *Distinguishing the Middle from Extremes*.[13] Mipham introduces
the original stanzas within the framework of a traditional "topical outline" (*sa bcad*)[14] and, for each section of verses, the text of Mipham's actual
explanation follows both the verses and Shenga's commentary to them.[15]

Mipham, a direct disciple of both Khyentse and Kongtrul, wrote on all
aspects of sūtra, mantra and the general fields of learning. As a whole, his
comprehensive authorship can be seen as a celebration of the principles of
clarity and depth, for with little patience for those who "talk much but say
little,"[16] Mipham writes with a natural elegance that centers on key points
(*gnad*). In the *Garland of Radiant Light*, Mipham relies on Vasubandhu
and Sthiramati to present the root-verses in a way that is both accessible
and in touch with the classical commentators. Shenga's commentary, with
its strong focus on the wording of the verses and its wish to present that
basis from which all commentarial traditions grow, leaves many issues
wide open to further interpretation. Mipham, on other hand, generally
goes much further, seeking to explain and provide clear solutions. This
marked difference in method makes, we believe, the two commentaries
excellent companions. While Shenga's commentary maintains a unique

closeness to both the root-verses and their very first commentary—a feature that necessarily would be lost in any other format—Mipham invites us to follow him on a journey of exploration, taking up the issues set forth in the verses and offering his understanding of them. We hope that the synergy that we have felt between the root-verses and the two commentaries might also be sensed in the translations.

ON THE CREATION OF THIS BOOK

During the fall semester of 2004, Khenpo Jampa Donden lectured on *Distinguishing the Middle from Extremes* at Kathmandu University, Centre for Buddhist Studies at Rangjung Yeshe Institute. Jampa Donden engagingly taught Shenga's commentary (for which I had prepared a draft translation) and based his explanations on the *Garland of Radiant Light*. Naturally, the wish for a translation of Mipham's commentary manifested. On Chökyi Nyima Rinpoche's recommendation, a group of translators was then formed, consisting of faculty and senior students at the Centre. The translators—Cortland Dahl, Catherine Dalton, Ryan Damron, Hillary Herdman, Nir Levi, Matthew Stephensen, and Beatrice Volt—shared the text between them. Working closely together with our Khenpo, they soon produced an English draft translation. I then collected the individual contributions and compared them against the Tibetan. Finally, both commentaries were edited by Cortland Dahl. Artwork and layout for the book was guided by Rafael Ortet.

Apart from Jampa Donden, we are also indebted to the Khenpos Sherab Sangpo and Sherab Dorje for their expert assistance. In our work it has been particularly helpful to have access to Richard Stanley's translations and text critical remarks, as well as the Sanskrit edition of Vasubandhu's commentary prepared by Gadjin Nagao. Among other useful features, Nagao's edition contains elaborate glossaries that compare the extant Sanskrit manuscript with Yeshe Dé's Tibetan translation. As an appendix to this book we include two glossaries: English-Tibetan and Tibetan-English-Sanskrit. In the latter, the Sanskrit entries have almost exclusively been extracted from Nagao's much larger glossary. Where a word in the glossary appears only in Mipham's commentary, and therefore has no explicit Sanskrit equivalent in Vasubandhu's commentary, we have marked the Sanskrit entry with an asterisk.[17] For the sake of general consistency, we have also in our numbering of the root stanzas followed the approach suggested by Nagao.[18] Many thanks are due to Mattia Salvini and Min

Bahadur Shakya for their valuable assistance in Sanskrit related issues, to professor John Makransky, Gillian Parrish, and Kathy Morris for their insightful advice, to professor Ulrich Pagel and Denise Till for sharing translations and research materials, and to the Tsadra Foundation for providing the visual representation of Mipham's outline on p. 166. We would also like to express our gratitude to George MacDonald, the great benefactor of Ka-Nying Shedrub Ling Monastery, for his generous sponsorship of the project. For those wishing to read the translations alongside the Tibetan originals, cross-referenced editions of the Tibetan texts are available for download at the website of the Dharmachakra Translation Committee (www.dharmachakra.net).

Distinguishing the Middle from Extremes is a true classic of Mahāyāna Buddhism that has inspired rich and diverse commentarial traditions throughout South, Central, and East Asia.[19] We sincerely regret all flaws and imperfections this attempt at translation may contain. In spite of any shortcomings, it is hoped that this book may still provide a useful link for those wishing to access these seminal teachings and the great wisdom traditions that they have inspired. May any virtue achieved from producing this book become a cause of genuine goodness everywhere, and may it serve to ensure the full and continuous presence of our precious masters.

On behalf of the translation team,
Thomas H. Doctor, in the spring of 2006

མདྷྱནྟབིབཾགྐཱ རིབཱིསཾ པྟུབྲྀྒྐཱནཱཾ བིཀརྟི ས༄
དབུས་དང་མཐའ་རྣམ་པར་འབྱེད་པའི་ཚིག་ལེཽར་བྱས་པའི་མཆན་
འགྲེལ་ཞེས་བྱ་བ་བཞུགས་སོ

རྒྱྲྀྨཱངྟཱནཱཾ མདྷྱནྟབིྲྀནཱཾགྐཱ བཱྱཱརྱཿ ཌྱཱྱཿ ཝཱྀཀཱ བིཀཏི ས༄
དབུས་དང་མཐའ་རྣམ་པར་འབྱེད་པའི་བསྟན་བཅོས་ཀྱི་འགྲེལ་བ་
འོད་ཟེར་ཕྲེང་བ་ཞེས་བྱ་བ་བཞུགས་སོ

MAITREYA'S
DISTINGUISHING THE MIDDLE
FROM EXTREMES

elucidated by

SHENPHEN NANGWA

Annotation-commentary on the Stanzas
on Distinguishing the Middle from Extremes

and

JU MIPHAM

Garland of Radiant Light — A Commentary
on the Treatise Distinguishing the Middle from Extremes

The light rays of your love pervade the entire expanse of space,
Awakening the intelligence of wandering beings.
Homage to you, Victorious One, Kinsman of the Sun,[20]
And to your spiritual heirs, Maitreya and Mañjuśrī.

Here I shall correctly explain the words and meanings
Of *Distinguishing the Middle from Extremes*—a treatise unconfined
By the extremes of existence, non-existence, permanence and
   annihilation;
An approach that reveals the genuine, excellent path of the noble
   ones.

Distinguishing the Middle from Extremes is one of the five great treatises of the Regent,[21] the supreme Bodhisattva of the tenth ground. It explains the profound key points of the entire path of the Great and Lesser
Vehicles and reveals reality, free of dualistic extremes. The treatise will be
explained under four headings:

1) The meaning of the title
2) The translator's homage
3) The meaning of the scripture
4) The meaning of the conclusion

THE TITLE

In the Indian language: *Madhyāntavibhāgakārikā.*
In the Tibetan language: *Stanzas on Distinguishing the Middle
from Extremes.*[22]

The first topic addresses the meaning of the title. When translated, the
Sanskrit term *madhyānta* becomes "middle and extremes."[23] *Vibhāga*[24] is
translated as "distinguishing"[25] and *kārikā* as "stanzas on."[26] Thus, it is the

treatise that correctly "distinguishes" the "extremes" of permanence and annihilation from the "middle"—reality free from extremes. "Stanzas on" specifies that the entire text is composed in verse.

THE TRANSLATOR'S HOMAGE

On the second topic, the treatise states:

> Homage to the youthful Mañjuśrī!

THE MEANING OF THE SCRIPTURE

The third topic is the meaning of the scripture, which includes two divisions:

1) A summary using headings
2) A detailed explanation of the meaning of these headings

SUMMARY

On the first topic, the treatise states:

> **Characteristics, obscurations,**
> **Reality, cultivation of remedies,**
> **The bases for this, attainment of the fruition,**
> **And the Unsurpassable Vehicle.**

[The treatise] opens by presenting the body of the treatise: **characteristics, obscurations, reality,** the **cultivation of remedies, the bases for this** cultivation, **attainment of the fruition, and the Unsurpassable Vehicle.**

The entire meaning of the text, from beginning to end, is grouped into seven topics. The characteristics of thorough affliction and complete purification are the first topic and are what is to be comprehended. Obscurations, the second topic, are taught next, as their elimination leads to the attainment of complete purification. The third topic is reality, which when observed brings about the elimination of these obscurations. The way in which the remedies are cultivated in relation to the observation of reality is taught as the fourth topic. The fifth topic is comprised of the occasions when the remedies arise in one's mind stream, while the sixth concerns the fruition that is achieved by cultivating these remedies. The seventh topic concerns the unique path that leads to the attainment of buddhahood, which is taught by highlighting the distinctive features of the unsurpassed vehicle.

Detailed Explanation

The second section contains a detailed explanation of these seven topics. This includes:

1) A general perspective on that which is to be understood
2) The unique approach of the Great Vehicle

The general perspective on objects of cognition is further divided into:

1) The objects that are cognized
2) The path of practice
3) The fruition of the path

The discussion of the objects that are cognized covers:

1) The characteristics of objects of cognition
2) The obscurations that are eliminated
3) The reality that is realized

The first of these, the characteristics of objects of cognition, is divided into:

1) The characteristics of thorough affliction
2) The characteristics of complete purification

The characteristics of thorough affliction are discussed in terms of:

1) The essence of thorough affliction
2) How affliction occurs

The first topic, the essence of thorough affliction, includes:

  1) A consideration of the way things are
  2) A consideration of the way things appear
  3) How to apply these principles

ONE
THE CHARACTERISTICS

THE CHARACTERISTICS OF THOROUGH AFFLICTION

The Way Things Are

On the first topic, the treatise states:

> The false imagination exists.
> In it, the two do not exist.
> Emptiness exists here,
> And within it, that exists as well. [I.1]
>
> Not empty, not not empty—
> This explains it all,
> Because of existence, non-existence, and existence.
> This is the path of the Middle Way. [I.2]

The explanation begins with the characteristics. **The false imagination**, the conception of apprehended and apprehender, **exists**. **In it, the two**, apprehended and apprehender, **do not exist**. The **emptiness** of apprehended and apprehender **exists here** in the false imagination, **and within it** (the emptiness), **that** (the false imagination) **exists as well**. Thus, in exact accordance with reality, it can be seen that when something is absent within something else, then the latter is empty of the former.

Emptiness and the false imagination are **not empty**, yet they are **not not empty** of apprehended and apprehender either. **This explains**

it all, both the conditioned, which is referred to as the "false imagination," and the unconditioned, which is referred to as "empty." **Because of** the **existence** of the false imagination, the **non-existence** of apprehended and apprehender, **and** the **existence** of emptiness, there is nothing that is unequivocally either empty or not empty. **This is the path of the Middle Way.** Thus, these verses accord with statements from the *Transcendent Knowledge* and other sources, such as: "All of this is neither empty, nor not empty."

It is said that the false imagination alone is the basis for all the appearances that occur within the context of this seemingly impure cyclic existence, and that it exists substantially. Thus, the appearances of cyclic existence undeniably arise; nobody can negate their mere appearance. But they arise through the power of our own imagination and do not have the least bit of establishment apart from that. Therefore, because conventions should not be denigrated, cyclic existence itself is held to exist by the power of the imagination. This is also referred to as the "impure dependent nature."

The apprehended and apprehender that appear to the imagination, the dependent consciousness, are not established, nor do they exist the way they appear. Like the perspective of high and low in a painting or a cairn that appears to be a person, they are purely imaginary and have no essence of their own. Therefore, that emptiness, the absence of apprehended and apprehender, is thoroughly established. It exists here, in the imagination, the dependent consciousness, as its intrinsic nature.

Within that emptiness, the imagination exists as well as that which possesses the property of emptiness. Just like fire and its heat, the imagination and emptiness cannot be separated, as they are phenomena and the nature of phenomena. This is so even when there is no realization. Once realization has occurred, they arise as the wakefulness that exclusively sees the nature of things. Therefore, the imagination is not exclusively empty. Its existence is substantial or, in other words, not deceptive at [the level of] convention. However, although it exists, the apprehended and apprehender do not exist as they appear. Therefore, neither is it not empty.

It is with this intent that sūtras, such as those of the *Transcendent Knowledge*, state: "All of this is neither empty, nor not empty." In this way, such teachings explicitly refute all extremes; their explanation is not one-sided. Moreover, as Vasubandhu says in his commentary:

Thus, in exact accordance with reality, it can be seen that when something is absent within something else, then the latter is empty of the former. That which remains present is, then, in exact accordance with reality, fully understood to exist there. This shows the characteristic of emptiness without error.

Accordingly, in the context of a discerning knowledge that properly distinguishes existence from non-existence, we may explain the following. When a rope is mistaken for a snake, the rope itself is empty of any actual snake. Likewise, the false imagination, i.e., the dualistic appearance of apprehended and apprehender, itself exists, despite the real non-existence of such duality. That which does not exist is the duality of apprehended and apprehender. Though that is how it appears to be, no such duality has ever been present. Thus, the imagination should be understood to be empty of the duality of apprehended and apprehender. Even though there is no snake, the rope itself exists conventionally and the very absence of snake is present in the rope. Likewise, that which remains present is the conventional imagination, as well as the thoroughly established emptiness that exists as its intrinsic nature.

These two must be asserted and accepted to be existent. If one asserts the non-existence of the imagination, cyclic existence will become absolutely non-existent and one will incur the fault of denigrating conventions. If one refutes emptiness, failing to comprehend that it exists in terms of its being established in relation to that subject, the imagination, then the apprehended and apprehender will end up being existent and one will incur the fault of exaggerating their status as ultimate. Therefore, one must know how to assert unequivocally what is to be negated and what should be established conventionally. Otherwise, one will fail to do so and end up asserting the opposite [of what is actually the case].[27]

When the false imagination, the mere awareness of dualistic appearances, occurs within cyclic existence, these directly perceived appearances exist in an undeceiving way from the perspective of that which experiences them. However, the apparent separation between the apprehended and apprehender is not actually present. And yet that emptiness, the absence of apprehended and apprehender, *is* present in the subject, the false imagination, as its intrinsic nature. Hence, this is ascertained to be the nature of appearance that lacks essential establishment, the unity of appearance and emptiness. This type of realization transcends the extremes of superimposed existence and non-existence—it is the path of the Middle Way. As such, it is the perfect realization of the intrinsic nature of entities.

THE WAY THINGS APPEAR

On the second topic, the treatise states:

> Appearing as objects, sentient beings, the self
> And awareness, consciousness arises.
> Its objects do not exist.
> Therefore, it does not exist either. [I.3]

> Thus, the false imagination is established.
> This is not how it is,
> Yet it is not absolutely nothing either.
> Liberation is held to follow its exhaustion. [I.4]

Having thus demonstrated the characteristics of existence and non-existence, the specific characteristics of the false imagination are now set forth. **Appearing as objects**, such as form, as **sentient beings**, i.e., the five faculties in one's own and others' stream of being, as **the self**, the defiled mental cognition associated with the delusion of self and so on, **and** as **awareness**, the six consciousnesses, **consciousness arises**. **Its objects**, the appearances of objects and sentient beings, **do not exist**. **Therefore**, since the appearances of self and awareness are mistaken appearances, **it**, the apprehender, **does not exist either**.

Thus, the false imagination is established because it does appear in this way. Nevertheless, because it is just the arising of delusion, **this is not how it** really **is**, and **yet it is not absolutely nothing either**. The reason that it is not held to be exclusively and absolutely non-existent is because **liberation is held to follow its exhaustion**. Holding otherwise, one would incur the fault of denigrating thorough affliction and complete purification.

What is the false imagination? It is the all-ground consciousness, which itself appears as the diversity of phenomena. It appears as external objects, such as form and so forth, as sentient beings endowed with faculties, such as that of the eye and so on, as the self, which refers to the defiled mental cognition, and as awareness, the six collections. Consciousness arises due to the power of the imagination's habitual tendencies and the apprehended and apprehender appear as diverse features like the appearances in a dream.

However, when these appearances are properly investigated, the objects apprehended by the six collections of consciousness are seen to be unestablished. The same water can be seen in different ways—hungry ghosts, for example, will see it as pus, while humans will take it to be water. Similarly, the "lack of establishment of external objects" is explained to imply that it is one's own mind that appears as objects, that objects do not exist at all apart from that which apprehends them. That being so, since the apprehended does not exist, the apprehender that is posited based on it does not exist either, because these two are not established separately but in mutual dependence. In this way, although the experience of apprehended and apprehender exists, this duality has no establishment.

This is what is meant when it is said that the false imagination is substantially established, that it substantially exists. If this dualistic consciousness were something that never knew any existence, like the horns of a rabbit, it would be completely non-existent and no one would be able to assert its existence. On the other hand, if it were dualistically established in the same way it appears, it could not be posited to be a *false* imagination either. This being the case, it is called a "false imagination" because it does not exist as it appears, as the duality of apprehended and apprehender.

Although duality does not exist, the false imagination is not something absolutely non-existent either because the experience of duality exists. It is not something that nobody has ever experienced, like the son of a barren woman. Categorizing the false imagination as a substance or as the basis for the concepts that occur within cyclic existence is itself a faultless tenet. No one can object to it.

The exhaustion of this false imagination, this delusion, provides for the attainment of the intrinsic nature, an attainment characterized by the absence of apprehended and apprehender. This attainment is asserted to be "liberation" because that which we call "cyclic existence" is not anything at all apart from deluded conception. Therefore, as the false imagination itself exists conventionally in this way, thorough affliction and complete purification, bondage and liberation, are all sound principles. If it did not exist, they would all be untenable.

HOW TO APPLY THESE PRINCIPLES

The third topic includes (1) a presentation of [the false imagination and emptiness] as the meaning of the three natures, and (2) how to access this meaning.

THE THREE NATURES

On the first topic, the treatise states:

> This, also, is the imaginary, the dependent,
> And the thoroughly established,
> These are taught with reference to objects,
> The false imagination, and the absence of the two. [I.5]

The characteristics of the summation—this summation being the three natures—is as follows: **This, also, is the imaginary, the dependent, and the thoroughly established. These are taught with reference to** the apprehending of **objects, the false imagination, and the absence of the two**—the apprehended and apprehender.

The imagination is presented using the principle of the three natures. These three are the imaginary, the dependent, and the thoroughly established. To elaborate, there seem to be external objects and there is a presence of dualistic experience. In this way, there seem to be objects, while [in fact] there are none. It is with regard to this that the imaginary, or delusion, is posited. These appearances are nothing other than the false imagination. Therefore, considering the basis for these appearances, the imagination's own essence is posited as the dependent consciousness. Finally, the duality of apprehended and apprehender is primordially devoid of actual establishment. Therefore, the nature of the [imagination] is explained to be the very essence of non-duality, which is thoroughly established.

HOW TO ACCESS THIS MEANING

On the second topic, the treatise states:

Based on observation,
Non-observation takes place.
Based on non-observation,
Non-observation occurs. [I.6]

Therefore, observation is established
As the very nature of non-observation.
Thus, observation and non-observation
Must be understood to be equal. [I.7]

The characteristics of the method that allows one to access the characteristics of the non-existence of the false imagination are as follows: **Based on** the **observation** of mere awareness, the **non-observation** of external objects **takes place. Based on** the **non-observation** of an apprehended object, the **non-observation** of any apprehending subject also **occurs. Therefore,** since there are no objects to be observed, the mind associated with **observation is established as the very nature of non-observation,** for when there are no objects to be observed there cannot be any observer. **Thus,** because what appears to be an object is [in fact] the very nature of non-observation, **observation and non-observation must be understood to be equal.**

The way to approach the nature of this false imagination, which is comprised of the three natures, is as follows. The very appearance of objects can be understood and observed to be the ripening of inner habitual tendencies. By familiarizing oneself with this understanding, one will realize that substantial external objects cannot be observed. In the same way, in not observing external objects, the apprehender itself will not be observed either. Therefore, when it is understood that external objects are not established, their identity can be seen to be that of the inner mind, as is the case with the objects in a dream. They are not observed or established as external objects, but as the very essence of consciousness. Thus, it should be understood that [certain affirmations, such as] "the observation that all appearances have the nature of mere imagination" and "the observation [that all appearances] are the essence of mere awareness," and [negations, such as] "the non-observation of external objects," are equal or similar in meaning. Although observation and non-observation are demonstrated from the perspective of affirmation and negation respectively, they are making the same key point.

HOW AFFLICTION OCCURS

The second topic, how affliction occurs, includes demonstrations of (1) what causes affliction, and (2) how affliction occurs.

THE CAUSE OF AFFLICTION

On the first topic, the treatise states:

> The false imagination is the mind
> And mental states that comprise the three realms:
> The consciousness that sees an object and
> The mental states that see its distinct features. [I.8]
>
> The first is the conditional consciousness.
> The second involves an encounter—
> Encounter, determination
> And the mental states that cause this to engage. [I.9]

With respect to the characteristics of its divisions, **the false imagination is the mind and mental states that comprise the three realms.** The first of these classifications, **consciousness**, is characterized by being **that** which merely **sees an object, and the** second, **mental states** such as sensation, are **that** which **sees its** (the object's) **distinct features.**

Of the factors that characterize engagement, **the first** is the all-ground consciousness. In being the condition for the other consciousnesses, the all-ground consciousness **is the conditional consciousness.** **The second** consists of the engaging consciousnesses and **involves an encounter** with form and the rest of the six objects. This includes **encounter,** or sensation, **determination,** or identification, **and the mental states that cause this** consciousness **to engage,** which are the formations, including factors such as volition and direction.

There is no creator of the afflictions that occur within the three realms of cyclic existence aside from one's own imagination. What, then, is this "false imagination"? It is the dualistic appearance of apprehended and apprehender, all of the minds and mental states that comprise the three realms. This explanation shows that the undefiled mind is not included in the false imagination.

What is the difference between the primary mind and its associated mental states? The factor that observes the mere essence of an object is called "primary mind" or "consciousness," whereas the particular way of apprehending in which one observes the distinct features of an object is referred to as a "mental state."

The primary mind, or consciousness, can be divided into eight collections of consciousness. Of these, the all-ground consciousness alone is known as the causal or conditional consciousness because it is the basis for the other seven collections. The second factor consists of the seven collections that arise from the all-ground consciousness and experience their individual objects. The divisions of mental states are as follows. Sensation is the experience of an object as either pleasurable, painful, or neutral. Identification is to apprehend an object by determining its marks. All of the associated formations that are mental states other than those in the preceding two categories, such as volition and interest, have the function of causing the essence of that consciousness to engage its object.[28] The mind, for example, is classified as a mental state of volition from the perspective of its moving towards and engaging an object, whereas from the perspective of its remaining still, it is posited to be an absorption. In this way, mental states are grouped into the three aggregates of sensation, identification, and formation.

How Affliction Occurs

On the second topic, the treatise states:

> Due to obscuration and to planting;
> Due to being led and to seizing;
> Due to completion and to determination due to the three;
> Due to encounter and to cohesion; [I.10]

> Due to being bound, due to the actual,
> And due to suffering—wandering beings are afflicted due to
>   these.
> Three and two are affliction.
> The seven come from the false imagination. [I.11]

The characteristics of thorough affliction are as follows. **Due to the obscuration** of ignorance that hinders seeing reality as it truly is **and** due **to** the formations **planting** seeds in one's consciousness that ripen the karmic habitual tendencies; **due to being led** by consciousness to a birthplace **and** due **to seizing** a body through name and form**; due to** the physical state being brought to **completion** by the six sense sources **and** due **to the determination** that occurs **due to the three**—the object, faculty and cognition—coming into contact with one another; **due to** the **encounter** that takes place when things are sensed to have either an enjoyable or a painful nature **and** due **to** the **cohesion** that arises as a result of the craving that sustains the consciousness impelled by karma; **due to** consciousness **being bound** by grasping to desire and other factors that are conducive to rebirth, **due to** becoming bringing about **the actual** acquisition of a future existence **and due to** the **suffering** of birth, old age, and death—**wandering beings are afflicted due to these.**

Ignorance, craving, and grasping are afflictive thorough afflictions, while formation and becoming are karmic thorough afflictions. The remaining links constitute the thorough affliction of birth. Thus, there are **three** [types of thorough affliction with respect to the links] **and** there are **two** further divisions that **are** also **affliction**s: causal thorough affliction and resultant thorough affliction. Of these two, causal thorough affliction includes the afflictive and karmic thorough afflictions, while resultant thorough affliction includes the remaining links. "**The seven**" refers to seven causes: (1) ignorance is the cause of error; (2) formations are the cause of implantation; (3) consciousness is the cause of being led; (4) name and form and the six sources are the cause of seizing; (5) contact and sensation are the cause of encounter; (6) craving, grasping, and becoming are the cause of cohesion; and (7) birth, old age, and death are the cause of sadness. All of these thorough afflictions **come from the false imagination.**

There are nine characteristics that summarize the nature of the false imagination: (1) the characteristic of existence, (2) the characteristic of non-existence, (3) the specific characteristic, (4) the characteristic of the summation, (5) the characteristic of the method for accessing the characteristic of non-existence, (6) the characteristic of division, (7) the characteristic of the categorization, (8) the characteristic of engagement, and (9) the characteristic of thorough affliction.

How does the imagination cause one to continue through cyclic existence and develop afflictions? The answer is that cyclic existence continues to evolve through the power of the unbroken relationship of the twelve links of dependent origination. What are these twelve? They are (1) *ignorance*, which afflicts wandering beings by keeping them from seeing true reality. In obscuring the perception of true reality, ignorance also functions as the source for the subsequent links, such as karmic formation, by grasping as if there were an "I" and "mine." (2) *Formation* afflicts wandering beings by implanting the seeds of subsequent existence in the consciousness. In this way, when the root text states: "Wandering beings are afflicted due to…," it should be understood to apply to all the remaining links as well, from consciousness on. Accordingly, (3) *consciousness* becomes infused with habitual tendencies and leads sentient beings to the place of their birth. (4) *Name and form* take hold of the body of one's coming existence. (5) *The six sense sources* bring the state of name and form to completion. (6) *Contact* determines the experience of an object based on the coming together of three factors: object, faculty, and cognition. (7) *Sensation* experiences the various types of enjoyable and painful karmic ripening. (8) *Craving* creates the cohesion necessary for a future existence. (9) *Grasping* totally binds one to such an existence. (10) *Becoming* brings about the actual acquisition of this birth. (11) *Birth* serves as the support for the suffering of old age and so on. (12) *Aging and death* is the essence of suffering.

In this way, wandering beings are afflicted because the twelve links of dependent origination arise in succession, the former giving rise to the latter in an unbroken continuity. Whenever defiling karma and affliction cause birth to take place, it entails changes in the psychophysical continuum (aging) and its cessation (death). By extension, nothing occurs but sorrow, lamentation, and so forth—this great mass of suffering.

By their very essence, the defiled aggregates entail suffering in each and every moment. The superficial appearance of pleasure is transitory and both pleasure and pain eventually become the cause of suffering. Thus, the aggregates relate to the three kinds of suffering: the suffering of suffering, the suffering of change, and the all-pervasive suffering of conditioning. In this way, they are the basis for suffering.

The twelve links of dependent origination can be combined into three categories. Ignorance, craving, and grasping are called "afflictive thorough afflictions," formation and becoming are called "karmic thorough afflictions," while consciousness and the rest of the remaining seven form the basis for suffering and are called "thorough afflictions of birth" or "of life." Furthermore, the term "thorough affliction" is used because all of these are rooted in the false imagination and repeatedly afflict sentient beings, binding them to cyclic existence.

THE CHARACTERISTICS OF COMPLETE PURIFICATION

The second topic, the characteristics of complete purification, contains two sub-divisions: (1) a brief presentation, and (2) a detailed explanation.

BRIEF PRESENTATION

On the first division, the treatise states:

> In short, emptiness can be understood
> By its characteristics and synonyms,
> By the meanings of these synonyms,
> And by its divisions and rationale. [I.12]

This passage shows how emptiness is to be understood. **In short, emptiness can be understood by** way of five topics: **by its characteristics and synonyms; by the meanings of these synonyms, and by its divisions and rationale.**

Emptiness is the basis for complete purification. It is free of cyclic existence, both in its causal form of karma and affliction and its resultant form of suffering. When summarized, this topic can be grouped into five categories: (1) the characteristics of emptiness, (2) its synonyms, (3) the meaning of these synonyms, (4) the divisions of emptiness, and (5) the rationale for positing it as either stained or stainless. Thus, it should be understood that the nature of emptiness can be ascertained via these five topics.

DETAILED EXPLANATION

The second division contains a detailed explanation. This section includes five headings linked with the sequence explained above.

THE CHARACTERISTICS OF EMPTINESS

On the first topic, the treatise states:

> Absence of dualistic entities and the entity that is the absence
> Of such entities—this is what characterizes emptiness.
> Neither existent nor non-existent;
> Characterized by neither difference nor sameness. [I.13]

How should the characteristics of emptiness be understood? The **absence of dualistic entities**, the apprehended and apprehender, **and the entity that is the absence of such entities—this is what characterizes emptiness.** The very essence of the absence of entities is **neither existent** as apprehended and apprehender, **nor** is this essence, which is empty of duality, **non-existent.** Emptiness is **characterized by neither a difference** between it and the false imagination, because phenomena and their intrinsic nature are not different from one another, **nor** by their **sameness**, because in that case it would not make sense for emptiness, once observed, to lead to perfect purity.

Emptiness is characterized by the absence of dualistic entities, the apprehended and apprehender, and the presence of the very entity that is the absence of these dualistic entities. When both the apprehended and apprehender have been negated through elimination, then emptiness, the absence of this duality, is established with determination because it is suchness. In this way, while there is no essential existence of apprehended and apprehender, there is no essential non-existence of that which is empty of duality either.

The subject, the false imagination, and its intrinsic nature, its emptiness of duality, are not characterized by being different or the same. Thus, the negation of duality becomes an affirmation of the emptiness of duality. If it were the case that the emptiness of duality did not exist, the duality of apprehended and apprehender would become existent, as a double negation is an affirmation. Furthermore, the emptiness of duality and the imagination are not of the same essence, because from the perspective of confined perception,[29] imagination is established by experience, whereas emptiness is not. Yet because emptiness is the intrinsic nature [of the imagination], they are not different either.

SYNONYMS

On the second topic, the treatise states:

> In short, emptiness implies the following synonyms:
> Suchness, the perfectly genuine,
> The absence of marks, the ultimate,
> And the basic field of phenomena. [I.14]

What synonyms should one be aware of? **In short, emptiness implies the following synonyms: suchness, the perfectly genuine, the absence of marks, the ultimate, and the basic field of phenomena.**

Emptiness is known by various names: suchness, the perfectly genuine, absence of marks, the ultimate, and the basic field of phenomena.

THE MEANING OF THESE SYNONYMS

On the third topic, the treatise states:

> Not something else, unmistaken, their cessation,
> The sphere that the noble ones engage,
> And cause of noble qualities—respectively,
> These are the meanings of the synonyms. [I.15]

How should one understand the meaning of these synonyms? Because emptiness is **not something else,** it is suchness and is, therefore, always present. Because it is **unmistaken,** it is perfectly genuine. It is, therefore, not a basis for error. Because it is **their cessation,** it is the absence of marks and is free of them all. Because it is **the sphere that the noble ones engage** through wakefulness, it is the ultimate, the object of sacred wakefulness. **And,** because it is the **cause of noble qualities,** it is the basic field of phenomena. In other words, observing emptiness is the source of all noble qualities. **Respectively, these are the meanings of the synonyms.**

Next follows the meaning of the five synonyms that were just presented. Emptiness is called "suchness" because it does not change into anything else; just as it was before, so it remains after. Likewise, it is called "the perfectly genuine" because it is the genuine, unmistaken way entities are. It is called "the absence of marks" because the nature of emptiness is the cessation of all constructed marks. It is called the "ultimate truth" because it is the sphere that the sacred wakefulness of the noble ones engages. It is called the "basic field of phenomena" because it is by observing this that all the excellent qualities of the path arise. Thus, it is the basic field, or the cause, of all noble qualities. These are the respective meanings of the synonyms mentioned above.

DIVISIONS

The fourth topic concerns the divisions of emptiness. There is (1) a twofold division, and (2) a sixteen-part division.

TWOFOLD DIVISION

On the first of these, the treatise states:

> **It can be thoroughly afflicted or completely pure**
> **And, thus, either stained or stainless.**
> **Like the element of water, gold, and space,**
> **It is held to be pure. [I.16]**

How may emptiness be divided? **It can be thoroughly afflicted or completely pure, and thus**, depending on the situation, **either stained or stainless.** One may then wonder: Well, since emptiness is in this way subject to change, how is it not impermanent? **Like the element of water** that itself is never polluted, **gold** that is never tarnished, **and space** that is never clouded, **it** remains free from adventitious stains and **is** thus **held to be pure.**

There are two divisions of emptiness. The thoroughly afflicted is called "stained suchness," while that which is completely purified of the two obscurations is called "stainless suchness." One may then think that if it is stained it cannot reasonably be of a pure nature. This is, however, not unreasonable. In the same way that the water element, gold, and space are completely pure in essence, suchness is asserted to be primordially pure in essence as well. There are no impurities in the way things are.

SIXTEEN-PART DIVISION

On the second of these, the treatise states:

> There is the emptiness of the consumer, the consumed,
> The body of these, and the fundamental abode.
> Moreover, that which sees correctly
> Is also emptiness. [I.17]

The divisions of emptiness also include the sixteen emptinesses. **There is the emptiness of the consumer**, the six inner sense sources; the **emptiness of the consumed**, the outer sense sources; the emptiness of **the body** that ensues from the transformation of both **of these**, which is the emptiness of the inner and outer; **and** the emptiness of **the fundamental abode**, the world vessel, which is the emptiness of the great. **Moreover, that** mind **which sees correctly** the emptiness of the inner sense sources and so forth **is also emptiness**. This is the emptiness of emptiness. The accurate perception of the ultimate is also empty—the emptiness of the ultimate.

Although the essence of emptiness cannot be divided, sixteen emptinesses are taught in consideration of, for example, different subjects, i.e., bases, of emptiness. These can be understood in the following way. The eye and the remaining five inner sense sources encounter, or take in, outer objects. They have no essential establishment. From this perspective, one speaks of (1) "emptiness of the inner." Similarly, the natural non-existence of the objects that are encountered or taken in, the six outer sense sources, is termed (2) "emptiness of the outer." The emptiness of the support of these outer and inner phenomena, the body, is the emptiness of all the bases. This is (3) "emptiness of the inner and outer." The natural emptiness of the fundamental abode, the world vessel that encompasses the ten directions, is referred to as (4) "emptiness of the great." These categories of emptiness are taught by differentiating the various subjects that possess the quality of emptiness. Furthermore, the subjective mind that sees that all outer and inner phenomena abide as emptiness is also called "emptiness." In this case the subjective mind is given the name of its object. Since that mind is not established by any essence of its own, it is called (5) "the emptiness of emptiness." The mind that accurately perceives emptiness to be the way entities actually are is said to be the "ultimate" because it is unmistaken. Because the ultimate itself is not essentially established, it is referred to as (6) the "emptiness of the ultimate."

> The objective of obtaining the two virtues,
> The objective of constantly benefiting sentient beings,
> The objective of not abandoning cyclic existence,
> The objective of preventing the dissipation of virtue, [I.18]
>
> The objective of purifying the potential,
> The objective of obtaining the marks and signs,
> And the objective of purifying the qualities of buddhahood—
> These are the objectives of the Bodhisattva's practice. [I.19]
>
> The absence of an entity, whether a person or phenomenon,
> Is, in this context, emptiness.
> The lack of such an entity is an entity and exists.
> That is another form of emptiness. [I.20]

The objectives of the Bodhisattva's practice are also emptiness. These objectives are as follows: They practice with **the objective of obtaining the two virtues**, those of the conditioned and the unconditioned. They also practice with **the objective of constantly benefiting sentient beings**, which corresponds to the emptiness that transcends the extremes of existence and peace. Cyclic existence has no beginning and no end. Its emptiness corresponds to **the objective of not abandoning cyclic existence** for the welfare of others. The qualities of virtue are not eliminated, even if suffering is transcended and none of the aggregates remain. The emptiness of this corresponds to **the objective of preventing the dissipation of virtue**. Nature means that which naturally is. Its emptiness corresponds to **the objective of purifying the potential** for buddhahood. The marks and signs of a Buddha are the specific characteristics. Their emptiness corresponds to **the objective of obtaining the marks and signs**. And, the emptiness of the powers and all the other qualities of a Buddha corresponds to **the objective of purifying the qualities of buddhahood**. These are the objectives of the Bodhisattva's practice.

The **absence of an entity**, whether it be **a personal self or phenomenal self**, is, in this context, emptiness—the absence of an entity. The lack of such an entity is itself **an entity and exists** as such. That is

another form of emptiness—the emptiness that is the very essence of this absence of an entity. Respectively, these two are taught to dispel the superimposition of persons and phenomena, on the one hand, and the depreciation of the emptiness of such superimpositions, on the other.

What is the purpose of meditating on emptiness? Its purpose is to obtain the qualities of the conditioned path and the unconditioned fruition, the transcendence of suffering. The essence of both of these is emptiness. Why, then, would one meditate on the emptiness of the qualities of the path and fruition? The two stanzas above present a detailed explanation in response.

One meditates on (7) the emptiness of the conditioned and (8) the unconditioned to obtain the two genuinely pure virtues. These two virtues give rise to the conditioned path and the unconditioned transcendence of suffering, the positive qualities of existence and peace. If one apprehends their marks and develops attachment to them, they will not become totally pure. If, on the other hand, one understands their emptiness and practices them without conceit, one will attain completely pure fundamental virtues.

That which transcends the extremes of existence and peace and is empty of its own essence is called (9) "emptiness beyond extremes." One meditates on this emptiness to be of constant benefit to sentient beings. Once the transcendence of suffering is actualized, and in such a way that one abides neither in the extreme of existence nor in that of peace, one will benefit sentient beings as long as space remains. If, however, one becomes arrogantly attached to this, complete purity will not be actualized. In contrast, it will be accomplished perfectly if practiced with the skillful means of non-attachment.

Cyclic existence has no beginning or end. Its empty nature is referred to as (10) "emptiness without beginning or end." One cultivates the knowledge that cyclic existence is empty so that cyclic existence is not completely abandoned. Unless it is understood that cyclic existence has no nature, one will see it as faulty and abandon it.

Those fundamental virtues that are not extinguished, even in the basic field where nothing remains of the aggregates, are referred to as "that which is not eliminated." Their essential emptiness is called (11) "the emptiness of that which is not eliminated." One meditates on the emptiness of the un-eliminated to attain fundamental virtues that are not extinguished, even when there is no remainder of the aggregates. Through the power of this meditation, the stains of apprehended and apprehender are purified and the body of qualities is attained. Thus, the fundamental virtues remain uninterrupted for as long as space endures.

The natural presence of the potential is called "nature." Its emptiness is termed (12) "emptiness of nature." One meditates on this emptiness to fully purify the potential itself, because when stains, in the form of a conceptualization of this potential, are purified, the potential will be actualized.

In this context, the signs and marks of a Buddha are explained to be the "specific characteristics." Their essential emptiness is called (13) "the emptiness of specific characteristics." One meditates on their emptiness to obtain the thirty-two excellent marks and the eighty pure signs. Once attachment to these marks and signs as being real is purified, they will be accomplished and completely perfected.

Here, the qualities of the Buddha are spoken of as "all phenomena." This includes the powers, the fearlessnesses, the unique qualities and so forth. Their emptiness is referred to as (14) "the emptiness of all qualities." One meditates on their emptiness to obtain the complete perfection of these qualities. This occurs by purifying the stain of taking the qualities of the Buddha to be real. The Bodhisattvas accomplish the path by observing emptiness in these ways.

The fourteen emptinesses mentioned here can also be combined into two categories. In this context, the absence of any entity in the form of a personal self or that of any other phenomenon is called (15) "the emptiness of nonentity." Here, the negandum, the two types of self, is negated by elimination. This emptiness, the entity that is the very lack of any entity in the form of the two types of self, is established with determination and exists. This emptiness is different from what was explained previously; it is termed (16) "emptiness that is the very essence of the absence of entity." The former is taught to dispel the superimposition of the two kinds of self, while the latter is taught to dispel the depreciative view that emptiness does not exist.

RATIONALE

On the fifth topic, the treatise states:

> If there were no afflictions
> All corporeal beings would be liberated.

If there were no purity,
Effort would be fruitless.
Not afflicted, yet not unafflicted,
Not pure and not impure. [I.21][30]

These stanzas on characteristics constitute the first chapter of the treatise *Distinguishing the Middle from Extremes.*

The rationale [for positing purity and impurity] is as follows. **If there were no** thorough affliction due to adventitious **afflictions,** then **all corporeal beings would be** effortlessly **liberated,** even in the absence of a remedy. And **if there were no purity,** then any **effort** to be liberated **would be fruitless,** even when a remedy is present. Therefore, since the mind is luminous by nature, it is **not afflicted, yet** since it has adventitious stains, it is **not unafflicted.** For this reason, it is **not pure, and** yet it is **not impure** either.

In short, the topic of emptiness is to be understood by this categorization of its characteristics. This categorization includes two characteristics, one associated with the absence of any entity and one with the existence of an entity. The latter, too, is characterized by being entirely free from being either an existent or non-existent entity; it is entirely free from being both itself as well as something else.

The synonyms of emptiness and the other classifications taught [in this chapter] are used to express the characteristics of emptiness itself, the characteristics of karma, the characteristics of thorough affliction, the characteristics of complete purification, and the characteristics of the rationale. Respectively, these are taught to pacify concepts, fear, laziness, and doubt.

From the perspective of emptiness, the way things are, the distinctions of pure and impure do not exist. Nevertheless, it makes sense to posit instances of being stained and unstained from the perspective of how things appear to sentient beings. If it were the case that there were never an occurrence of emptiness having adventitious afflictions, then there would be no afflictions from the very beginning and all corporeal beings would be free effortlessly. On the other hand, if emptiness did not manifest as the identity of complete purity and the experience of purity did not exist, it would not make sense for anyone to exert themselves on the path because such efforts would yield no result, even after cultivating a remedy. Thus, because the essence of suchness is naturally luminous, afflictions have no bearing on the way things are. The way things appear, on the other hand, involves the *appearance* of adventitious stains. From this perspective, there is no absence of affliction either. Therefore, the basic field cannot be one-sidedly explained as either pure or impure.

This was the commentary to the first chapter of the treatise *Distinguishing the Middle from Extremes*, the stanzas on the characteristics of thorough affliction and complete purification.

TWO
THE OBSCURATIONS

The second chapter addresses the obscurations that are eliminated and includes the following divisions: (1) a general presentation, (2) a detailed explanation, and (3) a summary.

GENERAL PRESENTATION

On the first topic, the treatise states:

> Pervasive, limited, excessive,
> Equal, perpetuation, and relinquishment;
> The obscurations are taught to be twofold. [II.1a-c]

Regarding the obscurations, the afflictive and cognitive obscurations possessed by those in the class of Bodhisattvas are **pervasive**, insofar as they prevent Bodhisattvas from accomplishing the welfare of both themselves and all others. The afflictive obscurations of those in the class of Listeners and Self-realized Buddhas are **limited**, as these obscurations only prevent the accomplishment of their own welfare. The **excessive** are excessive in the sense that these obscurations are manifest engagements with attachment and the other afflictions that occur in all three classes. **Equal** refers to engagements [in which affliction and its object] are proportionate, which can pertain to any of the three [classes]. This is obscuration in the form of latent potential. **Perpetuation and relinquishment** are obscurations that pertain to the class of Bodhisattvas, as they lead, respectively, to the perpetuation and relinquishment of cyclic existence, thus obscuring the non-abiding transcendence of suffering. In this way, **the obscurations are taught to be twofold:** those associated with the class of Bodhisattvas, those of the class of Listeners, and so forth.

Adventitious stains obscure the naturally pure intrinsic nature. These stains take different forms and can be grouped according to the mind streams of the individuals who possess them. The obscurations that are present in the mind streams of those belonging to the class of the Great Vehicle are called "pervasive obscurations" because they obscure the way in which those of the Great Vehicle accomplish the twofold benefit, their own and that of others. These obscurations are referred to as "pervasive," or "great," due to the fact that they prevent the accomplishment of the vast benefit of all beings.

The obscurations present in the mind streams of those belonging to the class of the Lesser Vehicle, the Listeners and Self-realized Buddhas, are called "limited obscurations." Unless these obscurations are eliminated, one will not attain the fruition [of this vehicle], which is limited in the sense that it [primarily brings] benefit to oneself.

The adventitious stains can also be classified with reference to how the afflictions arise. When intense afflictions like attachment arise towards an insignificant object, the term "excessive obscuration" is used, whereas an affliction arising in equal correspondence with an object is called an "equal obscuration." Alternately, "excessive" can refer to the predominance of a certain affliction, such as attachment, and "equal" to the three poisons being in balance. In either case, these two divisions are made in terms of the way in which the afflictions arise.

The cause of cyclic existence is perpetuated by the power of ignorance, while the relinquishment of cyclic existence comes about through intention. These [obscurations, in the form of perpetuation and relinquishment,] are posited to show what obscures knowledge and means, the essence of the path.

In this way, the first and last two among these six classifications of obscurations are factors that conflict with the path of the Bodhisattvas. The second consists of factors that conflict with the path of the Listeners and the Self-realized Buddhas and the remaining two are obscurations that inhibit the paths of both the Greater and Lesser vehicles.

DETAILED EXPLANATION

Second, the detailed explanation covers (1) the obscurations that prevent liberation, (2) the obscurations that inhibit virtue and the rest of the ten qualities, and (3) the obscurations that inhibit the three remedies.

The first of these topics includes explanations of (1) the actual obscurations, and (2) how they obscure.

OBSCURATIONS THAT PREVENT LIBERATION

THE ACTUAL OBSCURATIONS

On the first topic, the treatise states:

> There are nine characteristics of affliction—
> The bonds that obscure. [II.1d-2a]

Moreover, **there are nine** types of obscuration that bear the **characteristics of affliction.** These are **the bonds that obscure.**

Beginning with ignorance, there are nine factors that are characterized by being afflictions and which hinder the attainment of liberation. These afflictions, the set that begins with ignorance, are called "bonds" because they bind one to cyclic existence. As it is said: "Such bonds are obscurations...." Of these nine bonds, there are five that are not views: (1) ignorance, (2) desire, (3) anger, (4) pride, and (5) doubt. The next three—the view of the transitory collection, wrong view, and extreme views—are counted as one bond and termed (6) view. Belief in the supremacy of views [that are in fact mistaken] and belief in the supremacy of practices and rituals [that do not bring about liberation] are counted as one, the bond of (7) belief in supremacy. Finally, there are the bonds of (8) envy and (9) stinginess.

HOW THEY OBSCURE

On the second topic, how they obscure, the treatise states:

Disenchantment, equanimity,
And seeing reality;
The view of the transitory collection and its base; [II.2b-d]

Cessation, path and the Jewels;
Gain, respect and few material needs—
A full comprehension of these. [II.3a-c]

What does each of these obscure? The bond of desire hinders **disenchantment**, the bond of anger hinders **equanimity, and** the remaining
bonds conflict with **seeing reality.** How does this happen? The bond of
pride hinders one from fully comprehending **the view of the transitory
collection.** At the time of manifest realization, the pride of believing
"I am" arises either continuously or with interruption and so prevents
the relinquishment of this view. **And** the bond of ignorance hinders a
full comprehension of **its base,** referring to the basis for the view of the
transitory collection, because it does not allow for a full comprehension
of the appropriated aggregates. The bond of view hinders a full comprehension of **cessation,** because the view of the transitory collection
and extreme views create a fear of this, while wrong views cause one to
denigrate it. The bond of belief in supremacy hinders a full comprehension of the **path,** since something other [than the genuine path] is held
to be pure and supreme. **And** the bond of doubt hinders a full comprehension of **the** Three **Jewels,** because it prevents one from believing in
their qualities. The bond of envy hinders a full comprehension of **gain**
and **respect** because it keeps one from seeing their flaws. **And** the bond
of stinginess hinders a full comprehension [of the merits of having] **few
material needs** because it causes intense attachment to material things.
The bonds hinder **a full comprehension of these.**

The bond of desire hinders one from thorough disenchantment with
cyclic existence. This occurs because the attached mind perceives the defiling as having good qualities and, thereby, prevents one from seeing the
faults of cyclic existence. Similarly, anger hinders the mind from abiding
in its natural state of equanimity.
The remaining seven bonds all prevent one from seeing reality.
Specifically, pride hinders the knowledge of the shortcomings of the view
of the transitory collection, since it makes one fixate rigidly on the object
held in mind when thinking "I." Ignorance keeps one from knowing the

way the five appropriated aggregates are. These five are the basis for the view of the transitory collection. Ignorance prevents one from realizing their exact nature.

The bond of view obscures the actualization of the truth of cessation in the following way: The power of the view of the transitory collection, the view of the [personal] self, prevents one from reaching liberation because it makes one fear that the self might be annihilated at the time of cessation. The [extreme] views of permanence and annihilation, on the other hand, make it impossible to attain cessation. Wrong views cause one to denigrate cessation, thinking that it does not exist, for example. Consequently, such views hinder its attainment.

Belief in supremacy inhibits the truth of the path from arising in one's stream of being. Deceived by taking negative views and mistaken rituals and practices that do not bring liberation to be of paramount importance, one does not enter the authentic path. Doubt, being of two minds, inhibits knowing the qualities of the Three Jewels, as it prevents the arising of certainty. For as long as one is envious, being attached to one's own wealth and honor and unable to bear the prosperity of others, one will be unable to reflect properly on the shortcomings of wealth and respect. Stinginess hinders a comprehensive understanding of [the merits of having] few material needs. This occurs because it makes one cling strongly [to material things], such that however many belongings one may accumulate, one is never content. Unless these nine bonds are eliminated, one will be bound to existence and will not attain liberation.

OBSCURATIONS THAT INHIBIT THE TEN QUALITIES

This section contains (1) a brief presentation, and (2) detailed explanation.

BRIEF PRESENTATION

On the first topic, the treatise states:

Virtue and the rest of the ten are different. [II.3d]

It should be understood that the factors that obscure **virtue and the rest of the ten** [qualities] **are** a **different** [set of obscurations].

There are also obscurations that obscure virtue and the other ten qualities. These are different from those just explained.

DETAILED EXPLANATION

Second, the detailed explanation consists of three topics: (1) the thirty
obscuring factors, (2) the ten obscured qualities, and (3) an explanation
of their relationship.

THE THIRTY OBSCURING FACTORS

On the first topic, the treatise states:

> Not applying oneself, that which is not the source,
> And that which ensues from non-spiritual practice;
> Non-arising, not directing the mind in the right way,
> And the accumulations not being totally complete; [II.4]

> Not having the potential, lacking a spiritual friend,
> And feeling depressed;
> Not practicing and keeping the company
> Of negative people and those who are aggressive; [II.5]

> One's own negative tendencies, whatever remains
> Of the three and not having mature knowledge;
> Natural negative tendencies,
> Laziness and carelessness; [II.6]

> Attachment to existence and enjoyments,
> And a feeling of inadequacy;
> Lack of faith, lack of devotion,
> And taking literally; [II.7]

> Not holding the sacred Dharma in great esteem,
> Longing for gain, and having no compassion;
> Not having studied, or not having studied enough,
> And being untrained in meditative absorption. [II.8]

What are the factors that obscure virtue and the rest of the ten qualities?[31] (1a) **not applying oneself** to virtue, (1b) **that which is not the source** (i.e., that which is not a method for achieving enlightenment), **and** (1c) **that which ensues from non-spiritual practice** where the mind is not directed in the correct way; (2a) the **non-arising** of fundamental virtues, (2b) **not directing the mind in the right way, and** (2c) **the accumulations not being totally complete;** (3a) **not having the potential,** (3b) **lacking a spiritual friend, and** (3c) **feeling depressed** due to undertaking hardship; (4a) **not practicing** the transcendences, (4b-c) **keeping the company of negative people, and those who are** unappreciative and **aggressive** towards Bodhisattvas; (5a) **one's own negative tendencies,** (5b) **whatever remains of the three factors**—the obscurations of affliction, karma, and ripening, **and** (5c) **not having** the **mature knowledge** that comes from study and reflection; (6a) the **natural** (in the sense of inherent) **negative tendencies,** (6b) **laziness, and** (6c) **carelessness;** lacking full dedication to unsurpassable, complete enlightenment due to (7a) **attachment to existence, and** (7b) attachment to **enjoyments, and** (7c) **a feeling of inadequacy** when it comes to [engaging in] virtuous deeds; (8a) a **lack of faith** in people [who uphold the Great Vehicle], (8b) a **lack of devotion** to the Dharma, **and** (8c) **taking** the meaning [to be what is stated] **literally;** (9a) **not holding the sacred Dharma in great esteem,** (9b) **longing for gain** (i.e., holding gain, respect, and offerings in great esteem), **and** (9c) **having no compassion** for sentient beings; (10a) **not having studied or** (10b) **not having studied enough, and** (10c) **being untrained in meditative absorption.**

What are the obscurations that obscure virtue and the rest of the ten qualities? There are three factors that inhibit the kind of virtue that causes enlightenment: (1a) not applying oneself or, in other words, not engaging in virtue out of carelessness and laziness; (1b) not possessing the means that allow fundamental virtues to arise and develop, such as authentic scriptures, even though one has already begun to engage in virtue. Without such means, fundamental virtues will not arise and develop, as is the case when, for example, one is attached to negative treatises that do not provide the means for attaining enlightenment. (1c) It may be that one has studied and contemplated authentic scriptures and the like, but has not applied oneself correctly to spiritual practice and directed one's mind to their meaning. It may also be that directing the mind in a certain way does not serve to eliminate the afflictions. Such instances are referred to as "non-spiritual practice." The respective flaws related to meditation training, then, are "that which ensues from non-spiritual practice." These three factors keep one from authentically accomplishing virtue in such a way that it leads to the attainment of enlightenment. This occurs because (1a) one does not engage in virtue at all; (1b) one does engage in virtue, but does not possess the cause for developing it, i.e., genuine study and reflection; or (1c) even though one studies and reflects, one lacks the unmistaken key points of meditation.

The second set of three are (2a) not having the faith and diligence that allow the fundamental virtues that cause enlightenment to arise; (2b) falling under the influence of laziness and failing to repeatedly direct one's mind to enlightenment and its path in such a way that these fundamental virtues develop; and (2c) failing to integrate and, hence, totally perfect or complete the two accumulations, the cause for enlightenment. These three obscurations prevent one from understanding the fruition, enlightenment, and from cultivating the wish for it. This occurs because either (2a) the fundamental virtues that lead to the attainment of enlightenment are not gathered, (2b) one's mind is not directed in the right way, or (2c) the accumulations are not complete. Consequently, one is unable to embrace the process of developing the enlightened mind.

The next three are (3a) not having the potential for the Great Vehicle, (3b) not having a spiritual friend who will teach the Great Vehicle (though one possesses this potential), and (3c) having a spiritual friend, yet feeling depressed when thinking about the hardship entailed in practicing the Great Vehicle. These three factors prevent one from embracing the enlightened [mind] in a genuine way by putting it into practice. When they are present, one is practicing the Great Vehicle.

There are also three factors that prevent one from becoming an intelligent Bodhisattva, which here pertains to those Bodhisattvas at the level of inspired conduct:[32] (4a) not practicing the six transcendences, (4b) keeping company with negative people who cause one's enlightened outlook to degenerate, and (4c) keeping the company of people who hate or wrongly criticize the teachings and individuals associated with the Great Vehicle.

There are three more factors that inhibit [the attainment of] the path of seeing, the path that is achieved when delusion is absent and the character of the truths is directly perceived. These three are (5a) coarse expressions of the negative tendencies of one's own three gates; (5b) whatever remains of the obscurations of affliction, karma, and ripening; and (5c) not having the completely mature knowledge that comes from studying and reflection.

There are also three negative factors that do not allow the qualities of cultivation to develop, thus inhibiting the elimination of obscurations associated with the path of cultivation: (6a) "natural negative tendencies," which refers to inherent negative tendencies; (6b) laziness, i.e., not delighting in virtue; and (6c) carelessness, not guarding the mind from defiling factors.

There are three things that keep one from skillfully engaging in complete dedication. These factors, which occur due to one's limited concern and attachment to existence, are (7a) attachment to existence, i.e., the five aggregates; (7b) attachment to enjoyable objects like form; and (7c) feelings of inadequacy, i.e., thinking that one is unable to engage in immense virtuous conduct.

There are also three factors that arouse fear towards the Great Vehicle's profound and vast scriptures or inhibit an interest in them: (8a) lack of faith in people who uphold the Great Vehicle, or in its path and fruition; (8b) lack of devotion towards the scriptural teachings of the Great Vehicle; and (8c) mistakenly taking the words of such scriptures literally, not knowing their intended meaning.

The three things that inhibit one from teaching the Dharma without stinginess and without seeking wealth and respect are (9a) not holding the Dharma in great esteem and, consequently, not applying oneself to the sacred Dharma earnestly and wholeheartedly; (9b) craving material things or being strongly attached to them; and (9c) lacking compassion, the motivation to teach the Dharma to benefit others.

There are three factors that inhibit attaining the ten masteries: (10a) not having studied the Dharma, which comes from the karma of having abandoned it in the past; as a result, one remains ignorant about the correct spiritual practice. (10b) To have studied little, i.e., being unable to fully comprehend the vast scriptures and, thus, incapable of fully comprehending what to accept and reject; and (10c) to have studied, but not practiced and trained in meditative absorption using aspiration, diligence, and the other bases of miraculous power.

THE TEN OBSCURED QUALITIES

On the second topic, the treatise states:

Virtue, enlightenment, genuinely embracing,
Intelligence, absence of delusion, absence of obscuration,
Dedication, fearlessness, absence of stinginess,
And mastery—these are virtue and the rest. [II.9]

(1) The **virtue** that causes enlightenment, (2) **enlightenment**, (3) **genuinely embracing** the process of generating the enlightened mind, (4) **intelligence,** in the sense of becoming a Bodhisattva with knowledge, (5) **absence of delusion** and (6) **absence of obscuration** (i.e., relinquishment), (7) the **dedication** [of virtue] to the cause of enlightenment, (8) **fearlessness** concerning the profound, (9) **absence of stinginess,** and (10) gaining **mastery**—these are [the set of] **virtue and the rest.**

What do the thirty flaws obscure? They obscure (1) the initial arising of the virtue that causes enlightenment, (2) developing a mind focused on enlightenment, (3) authentically embracing the [mind of] enlightenment by putting it into practice, thereby (4) becoming an intelligent Bodhisattva, which causes one to (5) attain the path of seeing, the absence of delusion and, through this, (6) attain the path of cultivation, the annihilation of obscurations. Next, they obscure three qualities, respectively (7) the skillful means of dedication, the cause of the extraordinary path; (8) being unafraid of, and devoted to, the path and fruition of the Great Vehicle; and (9) teaching the Dharma to one's disciples without stinginess. Finally, they obscure (10) attainment of the ten masteries and the accomplishment of the final fruition of buddhahood. These ten situations encompass the entire path, from beginning to end. Once one has recognized what obscures them, if their respective remedies are then used correctly and they are eliminated, all the qualities of the path and fruition will be attained.

THE RELATIONSHIP BETWEEN THE OBSCURATIONS AND THE QUALITIES THEY OBSCURE

On the third topic, the treatise states:

It should be understood that for each of these
There are three obscurations. [II.10a-b]

How many factors obscure virtue and the other [qualities]? **It should be understood that for each of these** obscured qualities **there are three obscurations.**

The thirty obscurations are factors that conflict with virtue and the rest of the ten qualities just listed. It should be understood that each of these ten obscured qualities is associated with three of these. This has already been explained above.

THE TEN AGENTIVE CAUSES

> The ten agentive causes are those of arising,
> Enduring, support, that which is to be revealed,
> Change, separation, transformation,
> Conviction, understanding, and achievement.
>
> The examples associated with these factors are
> The eye, sustenance, the earth, a candle, fire, and so on.
> The others are the sickle, craftsmanship, smoke,
> The cause, the path, and so forth.

The reversal of these obscurations involves **the ten agentive causes.** With reference to their role as agents, they **are those of (1)** the agentive cause of **arising** or occurrence (for example, the eye in the case of an eye cognition); (2) the agentive cause of **enduring** (as exemplified by the four factors that sustain sentient beings); **(3)** the agentive cause of **support,** where one thing becomes the basis of something else (the world of the vessel for the world of sentient beings, for example); (4) the agentive cause of illumination, which is a means for illuminating **that which is to be revealed,** (for instance, a light that illuminates a form); (5) the agentive cause of **change** (as exemplified by a fire that can cook food and so on); (6) the agentive cause of **separation** (a sickle, for example, when involved in the act of harvesting); (7) the agentive cause of **transformation** (as exemplified by a goldsmith and gold); (8) the agentive cause of **conviction** (for example, smoke [that convinces one that there is] fire); (9) the agentive cause of **understanding** (an argument, for example, that is used to support a thesis); **and** (10) the agentive cause of **achievement** (as exemplified by the path associated with the transcendence of suffering). As explained above, **the exam-**

ples associated with these factors are the eye, sustenance, the earth, a candle, fire, and so on. The others [the remaining examples] are the sickle, craftsmanship, smoke, the cause of conviction, the path, and so forth.

The sequence of virtue and the other qualities is as follows: With the wish to attain enlightenment one must first develop fundamental virtues. Thereafter, the power of virtue must be produced and enlightenment attained. The basis for the development of these fundamental virtues is the enlightened mind, and the basis of that is the Bodhisattva. In order to relinquish error, the Bodhisattva must give rise to the unmistaken. Subsequently, having become unmistaken on the path of seeing allows the Bodhisattva to relinquish all the obscurations through the path of cultivation. Once they have been relinquished, all the fundamental virtues must be dedicated to unsurpassable enlightenment. After that, the power of dedication must be developed and, subsequently, one must become fearless concerning the teaching of the profound and vast Dharma. Having done so, the Dharma must be taught to others extensively and in an authentic way. One who engenders the power of numerous qualities in this way will quickly attain unsurpassable enlightenment and gain mastery over all phenomena.

These two verses are not part of the actual root text but were inserted by the great master Vasubandhu. He placed them in his commentary to clarify the meaning of virtue and the other ten factors. Their meaning is as follows. The first stanza shows what the ten causes are, while the second presents the examples associated with them. What are these ten agentive causes? They are (1) the agentive cause of arising, such as the eye faculty for arising of an eye consciousness; (2) the agentive cause of enduring, such as the four types of sustenance that cause the body to endure; (3) the agentive cause of support, such as the ground of the [world] vessel that supports its contents, [sentient beings]; (4) the agentive cause of that which is to be revealed or illuminated, such as a candle that illuminates a form in the dark; (5) the agentive cause of change, such as a fire that fries and cooks food; (6) the agentive cause of separation, such as a sickle for a bundle of grass; (7) the agentive cause of transformation, such as a skilled craftsman or goldsmith who can transform a bar of gold into various things, such as rings; (8) the agentive cause of conviction, such as the evidence of smoke whereby one ascertains the presence of fire; (9) the agentive cause of understanding, such as an argument that allows one to gain certainty about a particular meaning; and (10) the agentive cause of achievement, as when the transcendence of suffering is attained by [practicing] the path.

It should be understood that the eye and the rest of the ten things mentioned above are examples of the ten agentive causes, arising and so on. With this knowledge, one can then link these ten agentive causes with virtue and the other ten qualities. Virtue, in this case, becomes the agentive cause of arising because it produces enlightenment. Likewise, [the mind of] enlightenment is the agentive cause of endurance, as it makes the continuity of virtue endure. Genuinely embracing [the enlightened mind] is the agentive cause of support. It supports the very endurance [of virtue] and keeps it from degenerating. Intelligence is the agentive cause of illumination, as it allows one to comprehend fully the characteristics of cause and effect as they pertain to enlightenment. The supramundane path of seeing is the agentive cause of change, while the path of cultivation is the agentive cause associated with separating from the obscurations. Dedication is the agentive cause of transformation and fearlessness is the agentive cause of conviction in the Great Vehicle. Teaching the Dharma is the agentive cause of understanding. The ten powers are the agentive causes associated with the achievement of all good qualities.

With this knowledge, one will come to understand that the [thirty] obscurations hinder arising, endurance, and the other [factors that pertain to the ten qualities]. By reversing them, one should then gain a full understanding of the remedies that eliminate these obscurations. Thus, there are, for example, (1) engagement, (2) the source, and (3) that which is produced by authentic spiritual practice—all of which produce the fundamental virtues. Similarly, there are three factors, including developing fundamental virtues, that are the agentive causes associated with the endurance of enlightenment. This can be understood to apply to all the remaining sets of three as well.

OBSCURATIONS THAT INHIBIT THE THREE REMEDIES

Second, the discussion of the obscurations that inhibit the three remedies involves a brief presentation and a detailed explanation.

BRIEF PRESENTATION

On the first topic, the treatise states:

There are different obscurations associated
With the factors, transcendences, and grounds: [II.10c-d]

There are different obscurations associated with the **factors** of enlightenment, the **transcendences, and** the **grounds.**

The obscurations associated with the thirty-seven factors of enlightenment, the ten transcendences, and the ten grounds are different classifications than those mentioned above.

Detailed Explanation

Second, the detailed explanation addresses (1) the obscurations associated with the factors of enlightenment, (2) the obscurations associated with the transcendences, and (3) the obscurations associated with the grounds.

Obscurations Associated With the Factors of Enlightenment

On the first topic, the treatise states:

Lacking a thorough knowledge of the basis, laziness,
The deterioration of meditative absorption due to two factors,
Not developing, weakness,
Flaws that relate to view and negative tendencies. [II.11]

The obscurations associated with the factors of enlightenment are as follows: **Lacking a thorough knowledge of the basis** hinders the applications of mindfulness. **Laziness** hinders the authentic eliminations. **The deterioration of meditative absorption** obstructs the bases of miraculous power. This occurs **due to two factors:** (1) lacking intention, diligence, volition, or discernment, and (2) not having sufficiently cultivated the formations associated with relinquishment. **Not developing** the factors conducive to liberation obscures the faculties, while the **weakness** of these faculties obstructs the powers. **Flaws that relate to view** hinder the aspects of enlightenment from arising and flaws that relate to the **negative tendencies** obstruct the aspects of the path.

The four applications of mindfulness are hindered by believing that the bases for examination and ascertainment—the body, sensations, mind, and phenomena—are pure, pleasurable, "I," and "mine," respectively, and by lacking a thorough knowledge of their nature, which is impure and so forth. Laziness obstructs the four authentic eliminations. The four bases of miraculous power are hindered by a deterioration of one's meditative absorption, which is brought about by the presence of dullness, agitation, and other conflicting conditions, and a lack of conducive conditions, such as intention and diligence. Not developing factors such as faith in one's mind stream obstructs the five faculties. The five powers are obscured when, though one has developed faith and the other four faculties, they are not strong enough to resist their respective conflicting factors. The view of the transitory collection and the other factors discarded on the path of seeing obstruct the seven aspects of enlightenment. The inherent negative tendencies that arise from the three gates are problematic in the sense that they obstruct the eight aspects of the noble path.

OBSCURATIONS ASSOCIATED WITH THE TRANSCENDENCES

On the second topic, the treatise states:

> Factors that obscure affluence, the pleasurable states,
> Not abandoning sentient beings,
> The degeneration and development
> Of flaws and good qualities, attracting, [II.12]

> Liberating, inexhaustibility,
> Uninterrupted continuity of virtue,
> Certainty, and enjoyment of the Dharma,
> As well as bringing to full maturation. [II.13]

The obscurations associated with the transcendences are the **factors that obscure** (1) the **affluence** that results from generosity; (2) **the pleasurable states** that result from discipline; (3) **not abandoning sentient beings**—the result of patience;, (4) **the** respective **degeneration and development of flaws and good qualities** that results from diligence;, (5) **attracting** individuals to be tamed, the result of concentration; (6) **liberating**, which is the result of knowledge; (7) the **inexhaustibility** of generosity and the rest of the ten transcendences that results from means; (8) the **uninterrupted continuity of virtue** that results from aspiration; (9) the **certainty** about this very virtue, which is the result of power; **and** (10) one's own and others' **enjoyment of the Dharma, as well as bringing** sentient beings **to full maturation,** both of which are the result of transcendent wakefulness. These are the factors that conflict with the transcendences.

Stinginess hinders generosity, thereby inhibiting the result of generosity, affluence—the possession of great wealth. Likewise, faulty discipline hinders discipline, a cause that results in the attainment of the pleasurable states [of the higher realms]. Anger hinders patience and not abandoning sentient beings. Laziness obscures the diligent reduction of flaws and the development of good qualities. Distraction inhibits the attainment of meditative concentration, as well as using the four bases of miraculous power that rely on this concentration to attract disciples who lack faith in the teachings. Distorted knowledge inhibits the ability to teach the Dharma with the knowledge that liberates the minds of disciples. Lacking skillful means inhibits using these means to ensure that the fundamental virtues are not exhausted. Making aspiration prayers enables one to accomplish the uninterrupted continuity of all virtue. As this is the case, not making such aspirations inhibits this from occurring. Weak ability to overcome the factors that conflict with the transcendences obscures power and its function, which is to ensure that virtue will have a definite result and not go to waste. Factors such as not knowing the profound intended meaning of the scriptures and taking their words literally hinders wakefulness from arising, as well as its result, perfect enjoyment. Perfect enjoyment refers to one's own enjoyment of the Great Vehicle's teachings and also bringing all other sentient beings to full maturation by teaching them correctly.

OBSCURATIONS ASSOCIATED WITH THE GROUNDS

On the third topic, the treatise states:

> The universally present meaning, the supreme meaning,
> The supreme meaning of what is causally linked,
> The meaning that cannot in any way be apprehended,
> The meaning without distinct continua, [II.14]

The meaning beyond affliction and purification,
The very meaning beyond distinctions,
The meaning beyond development and decline,
And the bases of the four masteries. [II.15]

Ten types of ignorance relate to
The basic field of phenomena and are not afflictive.
These are the factors that conflict with the ten grounds
And they are remedied by the grounds. [II.16]

This section presents the obscurations associated with the grounds. On the first ground, one realizes the basic field of phenomena to be **the universally present meaning,** and in so doing achieves the equality of self and other. On the second ground, one realizes the basic field of phenomena to be **the supreme meaning.** By familiarizing oneself with it, realization develops further and further. On the third ground, one realizes **the supreme meaning of what is causally linked** with the basic field of phenomena. Thus, one understands study to be the supreme [pursuit]. Consequently, one will be able to cross through a fire as large as the three realms in the pursuit of one's studies. On the fourth ground, one realizes the basic field of phenomena to be **the meaning that cannot in any way be apprehended.** With this realization, even the craving for the Dharma is reversed. On the fifth ground, one realizes the basic field of phenomena to be **the meaning without distinct continua.** This allows one to see that there is no difference between oneself and others within equality. On the sixth ground, one realizes the basic field of phenomena to be **the meaning beyond affliction and purification.** Consequently, due to the meaning of dependent origination, phenomena are not seen in any way at all. On the seventh ground, one realizes the basic field of phenomena to be **the very meaning beyond distinctions.** Since there are no marks, the individual marks associated with the Dharma of the sūtras and so forth do not occur. On the eighth ground, one realizes the basic field of phenomena to be **the meaning beyond development and decline.** Having gained acceptance of [the fact that] phenomena do not arise, [one realizes that] the properties of affliction and purification are beyond development and decline. The eighth ground also brings mastery of non-conceptuality and pure fields. On the ninth ground, one realizes the basic field of phenomena to be the basis for the mastery of wakefulness, which is due to the fact that it is on this ground that one obtains the correct discriminations. On the tenth ground, one realizes that the basic field of phenomena is the basis for the mastery of activity because it is in the context of this ground that one works for the benefit of sentient beings by emanating in whatever way one wishes. **And,** thus, these latter three grounds are **the bases of the four masteries.** Hence, **ten types of ignorance relate to the basic field of phenomena and are not afflictive. These are the factors that conflict with the ten grounds and they are remedied by the grounds.**

The basic field of phenomena is what needs to be realized. Its essence does not contain different categories, yet distinctions can be made with respect to the subject that realizes it. This is due to the fact that the basic field of phenomena is perceived in an increasingly clear way during the meditative equipoise of each of the ten grounds. Nevertheless, there are no differences insofar as the basic field free from constructs is accessed during the meditative equipoise through the waning of dualistic appearances. When considered in this way, no distinctions can be made from the perspective of meditative equipoise, just as it is impossible to distinguish the individual paths of birds flying in the sky.

As the distinctive wakefulness of the meditative equipoise brings about progress from ground to ground, the discards of each of these grounds are eliminated. Through the power of this elimination, distinct types of certainty are experienced during the ensuing attainment that relate to the basic field of phenomena. It is from this perspective that the elimination of discards is explained.

Once the basic field of phenomena has been seen directly on the first ground, during the ensuing attainment the nature of the basic field of phenomena is understood to be pervasive and universally present. We may interpret the text to be saying that the equipoise has thus become the meaning that induces the certainty of the ensuing attainment, because it forms the basis for the attainment of that certainty. Alternately, we may take the word "meaning" to imply that the basic field of phenomena is realized to have the meaning of universality and the rest. Therefore, the obscurations associated with this ground are whatever hinders this realization concerning the basic field of phenomena, the universally present meaning. Because the wakefulness that arises on the first ground dispels these obscurations, this type of certainty arises automatically in the ensuing attainment.

Moreover, once one sees the basic field of phenomena directly, all phenomena are [realized to be] the nature of the basic field of phenomena. Thereby, the intrinsic nature of the equality of self and others is attained. All the following grounds should be understood in the same way.

[When compared to that of the first ground], the wakefulness associated with the equipoise of the second ground is an exalted and supreme realization of the basic field of phenomena. This is due to the fact that this wakefulness enables one to accomplish all of one's training with a diligence that is far superior to that of the first ground.

On the third ground, one realizes that scriptural study, the cause linked with the basic field of phenomena, is the supreme goal to pursue. With this realization, one sees that there is no cause superior to the study of scripture when it comes to realizing the basic field of phenomena. Furthermore, one also comes to see that this basic field is the most meaningful and perfectly non-deceptive amongst all that can be realized. Consequently, one becomes willing to cross over a pit of fire the size of the three thousandfold universe just to hear a single stanza.

On the fourth ground, one realizes that no phenomena whatsoever can be apprehended as "mine" and so forth. In short, one realizes that the basic field of phenomena is such that it cannot be apprehended in any way. Thus, if even the craving for the Dharma is brought to an end, why even mention the craving for non-Dharma?

The meaning that is realized on the fifth ground entails [an understanding] that the phenomena included in one's own and others' stream of being are not different from one another. Hence, one sees oneself as no different from, and equal to, the Buddhas and Bodhisattvas of the three times. In this context, the sūtras speak of a "tenfold equality regarding the purity of mind and intention." Through these, [the Bodhisattva understands equality in terms of] (1) the purity of the qualities of the past Buddhas, (2) of the future Buddhas, and (3) of the present Buddhas; (4) the purity of their discipline; (5) the purity of sentient being; (6) the purity of the Buddhas' dispelling views, doubt, and regret; (7) the purity of their knowledge regarding what is and what is not the path; (8) the purity of their knowledge of the path; (9) the purity of their settling in the qualities conducive to enlightenment; and (10) the purity of their bringing sentient beings to maturation. Through these, one realizes that, within the body of qualities, the continua of all the Buddhas are undifferentiated.

On the sixth ground, one sees the fact of profound dependent origination. This leads to the realization that there are no phenomena whatsoever that are first thoroughly afflicted and that later become completely pure. On the seventh ground, one comprehends the absence of marks and, consequently, realizes that all phenomena are, in fact, undifferentiated and of one taste. Then, on the eighth ground, one attains an acceptance of nonarising and realizes the fact that all phenomena abide in equality and that they neither degenerate from, nor develop beyond, this state.

The wakefulness of the three pure grounds realizes that the basic field of phenomena is the basis for the four masteries. The four masteries are (1) mastery over the non-conceptual basic field of phenomena, (2) mastery over pure Buddha-fields, (3) mastery over wakefulness, and (4) mastery over activity. To elaborate, on the eighth ground one attains the first two masteries. As one settles into equipoise within the one taste of the basic field of phenomena, constructs and marks are transcended and, thereby, one gains mastery over non-conceptuality. One also attains mastery over pure Buddha-fields, because countless maṇḍalas of Buddha-fields and retinues appear and are shown to others. In the ensuing attainment of the ninth ground, which follows the meditation on the basic field of phenomena in equipoise, one attains mastery over wakefulness, whereby one becomes able to teach the Dharma through the four correct discriminations. Meditating on the basic field of phenomena in the equipoise of the tenth ground enables one to attain mastery over activity in the ensuing attainment. Thus, activities manifest exactly as one wishes. In this way the wakefulness of the equipoise on these grounds is the cause, or basis, of these four masteries. Furthermore, since this occurs through the strength of wakefulness observing the basic field of phenomena, this basic field of phenomena should be understood to be the source of these enlightened qualities.

These Bodhisattvas are able to resolve the nature of the basic field of phenomena by seeing it directly, while ordinary beings can [only] understand it through inference. On the levels of inspired conduct, a slight certainty is indeed brought about regarding the significance of the omnipresence, lack of degeneration, and other qualities associated with the basic field of phenomena. Nevertheless, the grounds and their corresponding wakefulnesses encounter this pure basic field of phenomena directly and the force of this experience brings about an effortless certainty during the subsequent attainment, a certainty that cuts through superimpositions. Through this, an extraordinary perception develops that sees the nature of the basic field of phenomena with increasing clarity. This is the way to understand the process of progression through the various grounds.

"Extreme bewilderment" and "cognitive obscuration" are terms that refer to the ignorance that hinders seeing the nature of the basic field of phenomena as it is. In essence, this ignorance consists of the ten obscurations that are not, when considering the dichotomy of cognitive and afflictive obscurations, afflictive. These obscurations conflict with the wakefulness of the ten grounds. The remedies for these obscurations are the various grounds themselves, because once these grounds have been attained they are entirely eliminated.

SUMMARY

On the third topic, the treatise states:

> It is taught that there are
> Afflictive and cognitive obscurations.
> This includes all obscurations,
> Because liberation is held to follow the exhaustion of these.
> [II.17]

These stanzas on the obscurations constitute the second chapter of the treatise *Distinguishing the Middle from Extremes*.

In summary, **it is taught that there are afflictive obscurations and cognitive obscurations. This includes all obscurations because liberation is held to follow the exhaustion of these** two types. To elaborate, great obscurations are those that are pervasive, while lesser obscurations are those that are limited. The obscurations that prevent application are excessive. The obscurations of attainment are the equal, the obscurations of special attainment are those of perpetuation and relinquishment and the obscurations that prevent authentic application are the nine kinds of afflictive obscuration. The obscurations of the cause are those associated with virtue and the rest of the ten qualities. The obscurations that prevent engaging reality are those associated with the factors of enlightenment. The obscurations that prevent [the accumulation of] unsurpassable virtue are those associated with the transcendences, while the obscurations that hinder the development [of the transcendences] are those of the grounds. The summarized obscurations are those that are summarized into the two types [mentioned above].

As exemplified by the preceding explanations, there are an infinite number of obscurations that can be discussed, but in brief, these obscurations all fall into two categories: the afflictive obscurations and cognitive obscurations. The afflictive obscurations obstruct liberation and are the cause of cyclic existence. The cognitive obscurations, on the other hand, are explained to obstruct the direct perception of all objects of knowledge. In other words, they hinder the attainment of omniscience and cause one to fall into the realm of constructs.

That these two include all obscurations is a tenable position because there is no fruition to aspire to aside from liberation and omniscience, and the afflictive and cognitive obscurations are posited with reference to their preventing these two fruitions. What causes them to arise is the apprehension of the self of persons and phenomena, respectively, and it is the realization of the twofold absence of self that relinquishes this twofold apprehension. Therefore, since there is no superior ultimate reality to be realized other than what is realized by these two [insights], the types of obscurations are limited to a definite number—two. For this reason, it is asserted that once these two are exhausted, one will be free from all obscurations because no other obscurations exist.

If this is not accepted, one will fail to comprehend properly the final liberation in which all of the obscurations are relinquished. Neither will one be able to understand issues such as the remedies that enable one to eliminate these obscurations. Consequently, one will be unable to provide a solid explanation of the principles of the path.

This was the commentary to the second chapter of the treatise *Distinguishing the Middle from Extremes*, the stanzas on the obscurations.

THREE
REALITY

An explanation of the reality that is realized comprises the third topic. This includes (1) a brief presentation, and (2) a detailed explanation.

BRIEF PRESENTATION

On the first topic, the treatise states:

> Fundamental reality, the reality of characteristics,
> The reality of the characteristics of the unmistaken,
> The effect and the cause,
> The coarse and the subtle, [III.1]
>
> Consensus, the pure sphere,
> The summation, the division,
> And the reality of the ten types of expertise
> That remedy the belief in a self. [III.2]

Reality may be classified in the following way: (1) **fundamental reality**, (2) **the reality of characteristics**, (3) **the reality of the characteristics of the unmistaken**, (4) the reality of **the effect and the cause**, (5) the reality of **the coarse and the subtle**, (6) the reality of **consensus**, (7) the reality of **the pure sphere** of engagement, (8) the reality of **the summation**, (9) the reality of the **division, and** (10) **the reality of the ten types of expertise that** can be understood to **remedy the** ten types of **belief in a self.** These ten types of expertise relate to the aggregates, the elements, the sense sources, dependent origination, fact and non-fact, the faculties, time, the truths, the vehicles, and conditioned and unconditioned phenomena, respectively.

Here, it should be understood that all objects of cognition are included in the imaginary nature, the dependent nature, and the thoroughly established nature, and that reality is revealed by coming to an unmistaken and definitive conclusion concerning the way these three are. This includes the classifications of (1) fundamental reality, i.e., the three essential natures that subsume all phenomena; (2) the reality of the characteristics that reveal these three; (3) the reality of impermanence and the other unmistaken true natures, or characteristics, that pertain to these three; (4) the reality of the effect and cause of thorough affliction and complete purification with respect to these three; (5) the reality of coarseness and subtlety that pertain to these three; (6) the reality of consensus with respect to these three; (7) the reality of these three being or not being a pure sphere of engagement; (8) the reality of the five categories that are combined in these three; (9) the reality of engagement and the rest of the seven divisions that pertain to these three; and (10) the reality of gaining expertise that pertains to these three. Thus, beginning with the three essential natures themselves, all phenomena can be understood using the principles of these ten types of reality. The reality of gaining expertise has ten subdivisions. These ten function as remedies for the ten different views of the self that are to be eliminated.

DETAILED EXPLANATION

The second section presents a detailed explanation, which includes (1) that which is characterized, the reality of the three fundamental and essential natures, (2) an explanation of the characteristics of these three, and (3) a presentation of the eight principles that relate to them.

THE REALITY OF THE THREE ESSENTIAL NATURES

On the first topic, the treatise states:

> Three essential natures—the permanently non-existent,
> The existent but not exclusively,
> And the essential nature of existence and non-existence.
> Thus, the essential nature is held to be threefold. [III.3]

The **three essential natures** are the fundamental reality. The imaginary nature is **permanently** and exclusively **non-existent**. The dependent nature is **existent, but,** due to delusion, **not exclusively** real, **and** the thoroughly established nature is **the essential nature of existence and non-existence. Thus, the essential nature is held to be threefold.**

Fundamental reality is referred to as such because all phenomena, all objects of cognition, can be included in these three categories. It is also that which is resolved by means of the remaining classifications of reality. What are these three? They are the three essential natures, which are termed the "imaginary," the "dependent," and the "thoroughly established."

In their delusion, the minds of immature beings apprehend two types of self, yet essentially these selves are permanently non-existent. They have never known any existence and are, therefore, called "imaginary." The awareness that exists as the dualistic experience of apprehended and apprehender from the perspective of the imagination, yet which is in fact devoid of duality, no matter what may appear to be the case, is referred to as the "dependent." This is the basis for the arising of delusion, the imaginary. The reality that is the essential existence of the emptiness of duality and the non-existence of apprehended and apprehender is referred to as the "thoroughly established nature," the way things are. Thus, there are held to be the three natures, the essential natures of the imaginary, the dependent, and the thoroughly established.

CHARACTERISTICS OF THE THREE NATURES

On the second topic, the treatise states:

> Once they are understood,
> The exaggerated and depreciative views
> Regarding phenomena and persons,
> Apprehended and apprehender, [III.4]
>
> And existence and non-existence do not occur—
> This is what characterizes reality. [III.5a-b]

What is the reality of the characteristics? **Once they are understood, the exaggerated and depreciative views regarding phenomena and**

persons do not occur. This is what characterizes the reality of the imaginary nature. Nor do the exaggerated and depreciative views of **apprehended and apprehender** occur, which is what characterizes the reality of the dependent nature. **And** in the same way, once it is understood, the exaggerated and depreciative views related to **existence and non-existence do not occur. This is what characterizes** the **reality** of the thoroughly established nature. Being unmistaken about this fundamental reality is referred to as the "reality of the characteristics."

The exact characteristics of each of these three essential natures should be understood with reference to the way a subjective mind apprehends when in accord with what is fact. When a mind is able to acknowledge the nature of its object as it really is, without exaggerating or denigrating, then it must be apprehending the characteristics of the object as they actually are. Therefore, in this context, the characteristics of the objects [the three essential natures] are shown by explaining how a subject apprehends them.

What, then, are these characteristics? When the nature of the imaginary is understood, exaggerated and depreciative views do not arise. The former refers to the idea that phenomena and persons are substantially established, the latter to the belief that they do not exist at all, even conventionally. This is how the characteristic of the essential nature of the imaginary is explained.

Here, the subject [that experiences] a characteristic is referred to as [a "characteristic"], although the actual characteristic is the [apprehended] object. This is done to show that when the characteristic of a particular definiendum is set forth and subsequently understood, it is [always] done in dependence on the subject [that apprehends the characteristic]. A characteristic that is independent of, and separate from, a subject can never be established. Moreover, [the text] applies the name ["characteristic" to the comprehending subject] to make the profound point that no characteristics exist objectively as external entities, they are all simply set forth conceptually by the inner [mind].

The two types of self are not established, yet they do exist merely from the perspective of imagination. This is what characterizes the imaginary nature. It is how a mind that engages this characteristic in an unmistaken way understands it to be.

Likewise, when the nature of the dependent is understood, exaggerated and depreciatory views do not arise. The former refers to views that believe the apprehended and apprehender to exist independently and substantially, while the latter to the belief that they do not exist even conventionally. This is what characterizes the dependent nature. [The way in which this characteristic is presented with reference to the subjective mind, rather than the object itself,] should be understood in the same way as was explained [in the preceding explanation].

When the nature of the thoroughly established is understood, exaggerated views, thinking that the apprehended and apprehender exist, and depreciatory views, thinking that emptiness does not exist, do not arise. This is what characterizes the thoroughly established nature.

Thus, when the root text states: "Once they are understood…" in the context of explaining the three essential natures, the sense is that once the characteristics of these [three natures] have been resolved in a precise way, the negative mindsets that exaggerate and denigrate will no longer occur. Thus, it must be understood that reality consists of the specific characteristics of these objects; this is what the mind precisely determines once it no longer exaggerates or denigrates [the nature of reality].

THE EIGHT PRINCIPLES

The third topic includes explanations of how the three natures are presented in terms of (1) the true meaning, (2) cause and effect, (3) the subtle and coarse, (4) the meaning of consensus, (5) being or not being pure fields, (6) an explanation of the summation, (7) an explanation of the divisions, and (8) how they are presented in terms of the ten fields of expertise.

THE THREE NATURES AND THE TRUE MEANING

On the first topic, the treatise states:

> The meaning of impermanence is that of non-existence.
> It is also characterized by arising and disintegration [III.5c-d]

> And has the sense of being either stained or unstained.
> Respectively, these apply to the fundamental reality.
> Suffering is perpetuated, characteristics,
> And connection, which is held to be different. [III.6]

Emptiness is asserted to be the absence of entities,
This non-entity, and natural.
Absence of self is taught to be an absence of characteristics,
Characteristics that conflict with that, [III.7]

And its own characteristics. [III.8a]

How is this fundamental reality to be understood as impermanent and having the other [qualities associated with the truth of suffering]? **The meaning of impermanence is that of non-existence. It is also characterized by arising and disintegration and has the sense of being either stained or unstained. Respectively, these apply to** each of the three essential natures, **the fundamental reality.** Moreover, **suffering is perpetuated** by intense clinging to persons and phenomena, the imaginary nature. The **characteristics** of the three types of suffering, on the other hand, are the dependent nature. **And** the thoroughly established nature is also suffering, in the sense that it has a **connection** with suffering, **which is held to be a different** [form of suffering] than the above [two].

There are also three types of **emptiness:** Emptiness **is asserted to be the absence of entities** with respect to the imaginary nature, because the imaginary nature does not exist in any way at all. With respect to the dependent nature, it is empty in the sense that **this** lack of entity is itself a **non-entity,** for while nothing exists as imagined, it is not the case that wakefulness does not exist. **And** the thoroughly established nature, in being the essence of emptiness alone, is held to be **natural**ly empty.

There are likewise three types of **absence of self:** The imaginary nature **is taught to be an absence of characteristics** because it does not possess any characteristics. The characteristics of the dependent nature do exist, but since they are not as imagined, absence of self is taught with reference to those **characteristics that conflict with that** [which is imagined]. **And** since the thoroughly established nature is selfless by **its** very essence, it is taught to be selfless in terms of **its own characteristics.**

The defiling phenomena of cyclic existence are, in essence, impermanent and [entail the other qualities associated with the truth of suffering]. For this very reason, seeing them as permanent, pleasant, "I," and "mine" is a mistaken attitude. The objects of such a mistaken mind are also referred to as "mistaken," insofar as they have no bearing on [the actual nature of] entities. Their opposites—impermanence, suffering, emptiness, and absence of self—are their unmistaken, true character.

How, then, do the meanings of impermanence and the other [three qualities] apply to the characteristics of the three natures? The meaning of impermanence is applied in the following way: The character of the imaginary nature is one of insubstantiality. For something to be permanent it must always exist. The non-existent, then, is simply the opposite of something that always exists. It is from this perspective that the term "impermanent" becomes applicable to the imaginary nature. Permanent and impermanent are direct opposites; there can be no third category. Thus, the imaginary nature is referred to as "impermanent" in consideration of its not being permanent. The dependent awareness is characterized by momentary arising and destruction. For this reason, it is the [very] essence of impermanence. The character of the thoroughly established nature is such that it involves instances in which there are stains and instances where there are none. This is due to the fact that, from the perspective of the way it appears, the thoroughly established nature is related to that which is different from it. In this way, it involves instances of impermanence, which is why it makes sense to apply the conventional term "impermanence" to this nature. Thus, it should be understood that for these three reasons the term "impermanence" is relevant in the case of each of the three types of fundamental reality.

The characteristic of suffering [can be applied] in the same way. By taking the imaginary to be an [actual] entity, the various types of suffering are perpetuated. The dependent nature can possess the characteristics of any or all of the three types of suffering, [depending on the situation]. The thoroughly established nature is also presented as suffering. It relates to suffering insofar as it is the intrinsic nature of that subject. Thus, the way in which the thoroughly established nature is understood to entail suffering is different than was the case with the previous two natures.

Likewise, the imaginary nature is empty because it has no nature of its own. The dependent nature is empty because, though it exists, it is not the things it appears to be, things that are imagined. The thoroughly established nature is asserted to be empty by its own nature, for it is the very essence of emptiness that is referred to as the "thoroughly established nature."

Similarly, the imaginary nature is selfless because it has no characteristics of its own. The dependent nature does not possess any essential self because its characteristics do not match the way it appears, the way things are imagined to be. The thoroughly established nature is taught to be selfless due to its own characteristics; it is the [actual] nature of emptiness.

THE THREE NATURES AND CAUSE AND EFFECT

On the second topic, the treatise states:

> Thus, these are held to be the truth of suffering.
> There are also habitual tendencies,
> Origination, and non-separation. [III.8b-d]

> The essential, non-arising of the two,
> And the pacification of stains, asserted to be twofold.
> To be thoroughly understood, eliminated,
> Attained and actualized—[III.9]

> This is how the truth of the path is correctly explained. [III.10a]

Thus, these are held to be the truth of suffering.

There are also three meanings associated with the truth of origin: The origin of habitual tendencies refers to the **habitual tendencies** that are linked with the overt fixation on the imagined essences. The origin of **origination** refers to karma and the afflictions, **and** the origin of **non-separation** refers to suchness not being separate from obscuration.

The truth of cessation is divided into three types: **the essential non-arising,** the **non-arising of the two** (apprehended and apprehender) **and the pacification of stains,** which is **asserted to be twofold,** that of analytical cessation and of suchness.

How is the truth of the path presented as the three aspects of fundamental reality? The imaginary nature is **to be thoroughly understood,** the dependent nature is to be thoroughly understood and **eliminated,** and the thoroughly established nature is to be understood thoroughly, **attained, and actualized—this is how the truth of the path is correctly explained.**

The three essential natures encompass the entire meaning of the four truths, the fourfold summation of the causes and effects of thorough affliction and complete purification. As explained above, the three essential natures are held to be a precise presentation of the truth of suffering because they connote impermanence and its other three aspects.

Similarly, because the habitual tendencies associated with cyclic existence are accumulated by being attached to the imaginary nature, this [nature] is called the "origin of habitual tendencies," and because the dependent nature brings about cyclic existence, it is called the "origin of origination." The thoroughly established nature is not separate from this origination, in the sense that it is its intrinsic nature. Therefore, it is called the "origin of non-separation." In this way, the truth of origination can also be presented in terms of the three essential natures.

The truth of cessation can also be presented in terms of these three. The essential nature of the imaginary nature is that of non-arising. The apprehended and apprehender are unestablished, or unarisen, within the dependent nature, and the thoroughly established nature is the primordial pacification of stains. The latter of these three, the thoroughly established nature, is asserted to be both the basis for cessation, suchness, as well as the complete freedom from stains that is analytical cessation. Of these, the latter, the aspect of freedom, is actual cessation.

The truth of the path can be correctly explained in terms of the three natures as follows: The path engenders an understanding of the imaginary, in the sense that it allows the imaginary to be seen as a non-entity. Thus, it is taught that the name of the subject, the "path," can be applied to the object, [the imaginary nature].

The dependent nature is eliminated by means of the path. Enlightenment is attained by exhausting the dualistic experience of the false imagination. This was stated before when the characteristics of thorough affliction were being explained with the passage, "liberation is held to follow its exhaustion." Therefore, the dependent nature is referred to as "path," [yet it is actually what is eliminated by the path]. Hence, it receives the name of what eliminates it.

The thoroughly established nature is explained to be the path because it is that which is to be manifestly attained by it. In this case, the name of the cause, "path," is applied to its result, [the thoroughly established nature].

THE THREE NATURES AND THE SUBTLE AND COARSE

The third topic is divided into (1) the coarse relative, and (2) the subtle ultimate.

The Coarse Relative

On the first topic, the treatise states:

> Designation, cognition,
> And expression are coarse. [III.10b-c]

The relative and ultimate truths are the reality of the coarse and subtle. How should these be understood to relate to the fundamental reality? Relative **designation** pertains to the imaginary nature, relative **cognition** to the dependent nature **and** relative **expression** to the thoroughly established nature. All of these **are coarse.**

The three essential natures can be explained in terms of the relative and ultimate truths. The relative includes three divisions: The imaginary nature is relative designation, while the dependent nature is relative cognition. When considering the thoroughly established nature merely as an object universal[33] associated with the intrinsic nature, it is relative expression. The factors included in the relative truth are coarse, insofar as these objects are associated with the dualistic mind that is not in equipoise.

The Subtle, Ultimate truth

The second topic has two parts: (1) the actual ultimate, and (2) its divisions.

The Actual Ultimate

> The ultimate is singular. [III.10d]

The ultimate, in being the thoroughly established nature alone, **is singular.**

Only the thoroughly established nature is, by nature, free from dualistic appearances and beyond the thoughts and expressions of ordinary beings. It alone is the harmony of the way things appear and the way they are. For this reason, the ultimate truth, sacred reality, is the thoroughly established nature alone, not the other two essential natures.

DIVISIONS

On the second topic, the treatise states:

> There are held to be three types of ultimate:
> Fact, attainment, and practice.
> The thoroughly established nature has two aspects:
> Unchanging and unmistaken. [III.11]

There are held to be three types of ultimate: In the sense that it is an observed fact, the ultimate is asserted to be suchness, the sphere of engagement of ultimate wakefulness. Insofar as it is an attainment, the ultimate is asserted to be the transcendence of suffering. And as it is a practice, the ultimate is asserted to be the path.

How is the thoroughly established nature explained in terms of the unconditioned and conditioned? The thoroughly established nature has two aspects: As the unconditioned, the thoroughly established nature is unchanging, and in being the conditioned truth of the path, it is the unmistaken knowledge of the objects of cognition.

The second section presents the divisions of the ultimate, which are as follows. "Ultimate reality" refers to suchness, because this is the object of the sacred wakefulness. In being an attainment, the ultimate can refer to the transcendence of suffering, because it is the supreme pursuit. As a practice, the ultimate can refer to the path, since this is what enables one to accomplish the supreme fruition, the transcendence of suffering. Thus, there are held to be three types of ultimate.

In this way, all aspects of the ultimate are included within the three divisions of the ultimate ground, fruition, and path. Alternately, they are also included within the two types of thoroughly established nature, that which is unchanging, unconditioned suchness, and that which is unmistaken, the subjective wakefulness that realizes suchness. The first of these, suchness, is divided into two different aspects, the ground and fruition, while the latter refers to the ultimate accomplishment of the conditioned truth of the path. Hence, this latter division is making the same essential point as the previous threefold division.

From the perspective of this approach, the term "ultimate" is used to refer to all subjects and objects whose mode of appearance is in harmony with the way they [actually] are. This justifies the approach employed here, where the truth of the path is explained to be included as part of the thoroughly established nature.

In this context, the term "pure dependent nature" is also applied. It should be understood that this is done because of certain considerations and that it does not contradict [what was just explained].

THE THREE NATURES AND CONSENSUS

On the fourth topic, the treatise states:

> Due to one factor there is consensus in the world
> And due to three there is rational consensus. [III.12a-b]

How may one consider the fundamental reality in terms of the reality of consensus? **Due to one factor**, the imaginary nature, **there is consensus in the world.** Hence, all may agree that a certain thing is earth and not fire, or form and not sound; **and due to the three** validations **there is rational consensus.**

Every possible phenomenon is set forth in one of two ways, either by being consented to in the world or through reasoning. The difference between these two types of consensus is taught in the following way: When something is agreed upon as a convention simply through the application of a linguistic symbol, such as "pillar" or "vase," it is referred to as "consensus of mundane convention." "Logical consensus," on the other hand, refers to what is agreed upon by individuals who are learned in the field of reasoning. Such individuals posit certain meanings and agree on them by employing the validation of direct perception, inference, and scriptural authority, or, alternately, via the three reasonings of function, dependency, and intrinsic nature. To use an example, referring to something that performs the function of holding up beams as a "pillar" involves consensus by mundane convention. In contrast, saying that the pillar is emptiness involves consensus through reasoning.

With reference to which of the two types of consensus is the topic of our discussion, the three essential natures, agreed upon and established? Mundane consensus is set forth solely from the perspective of the imaginary. It is in the world that various labels are applied based on attachment to the way things appear. The dependent nature and thoroughly established nature, on the other hand, are agreed upon rationally using the three types of validation.

Alternatively, we may say that mundane consensus is based on the imaginary nature alone, whereas consensus in treatises can be set forth in terms of any of the three natures. Based on direct perception and the other [two types of validation], the treatises speak of numerous principles pertaining to the three natures.

THE THREE NATURES AND PURITY

On the fifth topic, the treatise states:

> **The pure field of engagement is twofold,**
> **Yet explained to be only one. [III.12c-d]**

The reality of **the pure field of engagement is twofold:** the field that is engaged in by the wakefulness purified of the afflictive obscurations and another associated with the purification of the cognitive obscurations. **Yet,** because the other two essential natures are not fields engaged in by the two types of wakefulness, it is **explained to be only one** [of the three natures], the thoroughly established.

The field that is engaged in by pure wakefulness is explained to be twofold: the field that is engaged in by the wakefulness purified of the afflictive obscurations and the field that is engaged in by the wakefulness purified of the cognitive obscurations. These fields are neither the imaginary nature nor the dependent nature. They are explained to be the thoroughly established nature alone. This is due to the fact that when these fields are accessed, the way things appear is in harmony with the way they are.

THE THREE NATURES AND THE SUMMATION

On the sixth topic, the treatise states:

> **Reason, conception, and name**
> **Are included in two.**
> **Genuine wakefulness and supreme reality**
> **Are subsumed as only one. [III.13]**

How can the reality of the summation be understood in terms of the fundamental reality? Beginning with the five types of being, **reason** and **conception** are the dependent nature **and name** is the imaginary nature. Hence, these three **are included in two** [categories]. **Genuine wakefulness and** the **supreme reality**, suchness, **are subsumed as only one**, the thoroughly established nature.

It is said that the entire meaning of the Great Vehicle can be condensed into five types of being, or five categories. What are these five? They are name, reason, concept, genuine wakefulness, and suchness. A name is a mere designation based on a linguistic symbol such as "pillar" or "vase." A reason is the basis for such designations, something that performs the function of supporting beams, for example, or which has a round-bellied appearance. Conception refers to the eight collections of consciousness. Genuine wakefulness is the subjective side of suchness. Suchness, in turn, is the basic field of phenomena that is observed by means of the path.

These five categories can be condensed into the three essential natures. How so? Reason, conception, and name are included in two categories, the dependent nature and the imaginary nature. Conception, the consciousness that has the nature of the eight collections, is included in the dependent nature, as are reasons, the appearances of various phenomena within dualistic experience that form the bases for designation. Names are included in the imaginary nature. Genuine wakefulness and suchness, the reality that is supreme among all qualities, are subsumed into the thoroughly established nature alone. As explained above, the latter two refer to the objective and subjective aspects of the thoroughly established nature.

DIVISIONS OF THE THREE NATURES

On the seventh topic, the treatise states:

> The twofold reality of engagement;
> Abidance and wrong engagement;
> Characteristics, awareness,
> Purity, and genuine practice are one. [III.14]

How is the divisional reality to be understood in terms of the fundamental reality? As taught in the Sūtra of the Definitive Explanation of the Intent, there are seven types of reality: (1) **The twofold reality of engagement** pertains to both the imaginary and dependent natures.

The realities of (2) **abidance and (3) wrong engagement** (or mistaken practice) should be understood to be twofold in the same way. The realities of (4) **characteristics,** (5) **awareness,** (6) **purity, and** (7) **genuine practice are one,** the thoroughly established nature.

The *Ornament of the Sūtras* teaches:

> The explanation of the truths
> Is based upon the seven types of suchness.

The suchness of engagement, the progression and reversal of the twelve links of dependent origination, is included within the pure and the impure dependent nature. The suchness of the characteristic aspects is the three-fold absence of essential nature: The imaginary nature is the absence of the essential nature of characteristics; the dependent nature is the absence of the essential nature of arising; and the thoroughly established nature is the ultimate absence of essential nature. That which is characterized [by these characteristics] is the suchness of awareness, the eight collections of consciousness. The suchness of abidance is the truth of suffering, the situation in which impermanence and the rest of its four distinct features are present. The suchness of wrong engagement is its cause, the truth of origin, which has four aspects, including full arising. The suchness of purity is the truth of cessation and its four qualities of cessation, peace, and so forth. The suchness of genuine practice is the truth of the path, which has four aspects: path, reason, practice, and deliverance. These seven are referred to as "the seven types of suchness."

Alternatively, when looking at both *The Sūtra [of the Definitive Explanation of the Intent]* and *Distinguishing the Middle from Extremes,* engagement is the continuous engagement in cyclic existence without beginning or end; the characteristics are the two types of selflessness; awareness is the understanding that all formations are mere awareness; and, as was just explained, the remaining four apply to the four truths.

These seven types of reality are based on the three essential natures in the following way: The reality of engagement is delineated in terms of both the imaginary and dependent nature. This is due to the fact that the engagements of cyclic existence come about because of two factors: (1) concepts of the imaginary being real, and (2) the essential [presence of] the impure dependent nature. Abidance and mistaken practice, or wrong engagement, are delineated in terms of both the imaginary and dependent natures in just the same way. As just explained, the causes and effects of cyclic existence are the workings of the dependent nature, as these involve conceiving the imaginary to be real.

The realities of the characteristics, cognition, purity, and genuine engagement are included only within the thoroughly established nature. It should, therefore, be understood that those four divisions are based on it alone. The characteristics and purity are associated with the unchanging thoroughly established nature. Respectively, these two refer to the fact of selflessness and to cessation. The realization that all phenomena are mere awareness, as well as the genuine practice of the path, are divisions of the unmistaken thoroughly established nature, as they involve correctly engaging the nature of things.

THE TEN TOPICS OF KNOWLEDGE

The eighth topic is divided into (1) the ten views of self that are eliminated, and (2) the ten fields of expertise that eliminate them.

THE TEN VIEWS OF SELF

On the first topic, the treatise states:

> **Singular, a cause, a consumer,**
> **A creator, in control, a ruler,**
> **Permanent, the basis for affliction and purification,**
> **Having a spiritual practice, [III.15]**
>
> **And bound and liberated—**
> **These are the ways of believing in a self. [III.16a-b]**

The reality of the ten types of expertise functions as a remedy against the ten ways of viewing the aggregates and nine other factors as a self. What are these views? A self is believed to be **singular, a cause, a consumer, a creator, in control, a ruler, permanent, the basis for affliction and purification, having a spiritual practice, and** [first] **bound and** [later] **liberated**—these are the ways of believing in a self.

The ten fields of expertise encompass all objects of cognition. The power that ensues from gaining this type of expertise, the comprehensive understanding of the nature of these ten topics, automatically brings about the elimination of the ten views of the self. What are the ten types of expertise? They are expertise regarding (1) the aggregates, (2) the elements, (3) the sense sources, (4) dependent origination, (5) fact and non-fact, (6) the faculties, (7) time, (8) the truths, (9) the vehicles, and (10) the conditioned and unconditioned. The ten ways of believing the self to be singular, a cause, and so forth are eliminated [by gaining expertise in these ten fields].

Gaining expertise regarding the aggregates eliminates the belief that the self is singular. The reason for this is as follows: The basis upon which the self is imputed is simply the five aggregates. This basis is in no way established as singular or partless, but is, instead, comprised of these five aggregates. Moreover, each of the aggregates itself has many divisions and is, thus, an aggregation of various phenomena. This is why they are classified as "aggregates." Comprehending this enables one to understand that there is no such thing as a "singular self."

Similarly, the idea that the self is the cause of the world vessel and its inhabitants is eliminated by gaining expertise regarding the elements. All outer and inner phenomena are included in the eighteen elements. Each of these is able to perform its own function, which constitutes its own distinct seminal capacity. Therefore, it should be understood that the vessel and its contents arise due to these distinct causes; in no way are they caused by a self.

The belief that the self is that which encounters, or consumes, is eliminated by gaining expertise regarding the sense sources. All phenomena are included within the sense sources; nothing exists apart from these twelve. The six outer sense sources are encountered by the six inner sense sources. Thus, it is realized that there is no consumer other than merely the inner sense sources.

The belief that the self is the creator of all things is eliminated by gaining expertise regarding dependent origination. Once the particular causes and conditions for their dependent origination have come together, phenomena cannot help but arise. On the other hand, if their causes and conditions do not come together, they will not. When this is seen to be the case, it is understood that the self does not create anything at all.

The belief that the self is autonomous and has control over everything is eliminated by gaining expertise regarding fact and non-fact. This entails the understanding that it is due to the various instances of fact and non-fact that all phenomena are experienced as either existent or non-existent, as being one way and not another. Once this is understood, the self will be seen to have no power at all to assume control.

Seeing the self as the ruler, as the one in charge or the central decisive factor, is eliminated by gaining expertise regarding the faculties. The twenty-two faculties alone have control over the qualities of thorough affliction and complete purification. Aside from these, nothing else is necessary to govern [their manifestation], nor is anything observed to do so.

The belief that the self is permanent, something that does not change or transform from the past to the future, is eliminated by gaining expertise regarding time. The three times are posited based on the arising and cessation of entities. Because there are three different situations, they cannot possibly be one. If something is an entity, it must arise and cease. Thus, it is impossible for something to remain unchanged throughout the three times.

The view that the self is the very foundation of, and basis for, thorough affliction and complete purification is eliminated by gaining expertise regarding the truths. The four truths relate to thorough affliction and complete purification. Of these four, two aspects are causal and two resultant. By understanding these truths, one is led to the realization that there are no other bases for thorough affliction and complete purification; there is nothing else that encounters [affliction and purification].

The belief that the self is a being that has a spiritual practice is eliminated by becoming an expert in the vehicles. It is the practice of the three vehicles' paths that makes the various [excellent] qualities appear. There is nothing aside from this that can be observed to be engaged in spiritual practice or training.

The idea that the self has the particular trait of being bound at one point in time and liberated at another is eliminated by gaining expertise about the conditioned and the unconditioned. Unconditioned analytical cessation, the exhaustion of defiling conditioned phenomena, is termed "transcendence of suffering." Aside from this cessation, there is no self that is impure at first and then pure later that can be observed by valid cognition. If there were such a self, it would logically follow that liberation is impossible.

In this way, those who lack expertise observe the aggregates and the rest of these ten factors and then go on to form beliefs about the self, imagining it to be permanent, singular, autonomous, and so forth. Discriminating knowledge, on the other hand, can be used to correctly resolve the nature of these objects of cognition, the bases of these views. This insight naturally liberates one from all negative views.

THE TEN TYPES OF KNOWLEDGE

The second topic has two sections: (1) the way in which the ten topics are included in the three natures, and (2) how to gain expertise in each of these fields.

THE TEN TOPICS AND THE THREE NATURES

On the first topic, the treatise states:

> **They are included as imagination, the sense of conception,**
> **And the sense of intrinsic nature. [III.16c-d]**

How are these ten types of reality, those associated with gaining expertise, included in the fundamental reality? **They are included as** follows: Forms imputed by the **imagination** are the imaginary nature of form; form, in **the sense of conception** and imputation, is the dependent nature of form; **and** in **the sense of** its **intrinsic nature,** it is the thoroughly established nature of form. [The three natures] are applicable to sensation and the remaining aggregates, as well as to the elements, sense sources, and so forth, in the same way that they are here applied to form.

The ten fields of expertise are included in the three essential natures in the following way: When [the objects related to] these fields are experienced and conceived of dualistically, then that which is conceived of constitutes the imaginary nature. Considering the fact that these [conceptions] are all, in essence, just awareness, they are the dependent nature. And considering the fact that their intrinsic nature is empty of duality, they are also the thoroughly established nature. In this way, the aggregates and the other nine topics are included in the three essential natures. For example, form that is conceived of and spoken about as an outer object is the imaginary nature of form. Awareness itself appearing as the thought of form is the dependent nature of form. The intrinsic nature of form is the absence of duality, which is the thoroughly established nature of form.

It thus makes sense to classify form in terms of the imaginary and the other two natures. This can also be applied to sensation, identification, and the remaining aggregates, as well as to the elements, sense sources, and the other fields of expertise.

HOW TO GAIN EXPERTISE IN EACH OF THESE FIELDS

The second section presents a detailed explanation on the ten topics set forth above. Of these, knowledge of the topic of the aggregates will be discussed first.

THE AGGREGATES

On the first topic, the treatise states:

> First, their character is one of multiplicity,
> Inclusion, and thorough differentiation. [III.17a-b]

Gaining expertise about the aggregates and the other nine topics functions as a remedy for the ten beliefs about the self. While this was explained above, the character of the aggregates and so forth were not discussed. These will now be presented. **First** of all, the aggregates must be understood to have a threefold character: **Their character is one of multiplicity** (as in the frequent cases where it is said, "all types of form, whether past or future"), one of **inclusion** (as when it is said that "all of these are included in…"), **and** one of **thorough differentiation** (as when the distinct characteristics of form and so forth are posited). The term "aggregate" [literally] means collection.

The aggregates are the first of the ten fields of expertise. When we speak of "aggregates," we are referring to multiple components that are gathered together. This term is applied with reference to two factors: (1) the various divisions of conditioned phenomena, each of which is comprised of numerous distinct and specifically characterized particulars, and (2) [the fact that] these various phenomena can be gathered together with respect to their being of similar class. What are the aggregates? They are the aggregates of form, sensation, identification, formation, and consciousness.

Form is comprised of the five sense faculties and their five objects. By nature, these ten are established as particles and are, thus, of a similar class in that they are suited to be form. For this reason, all such distinct phenomena throughout space and time are gathered together and enumerated as the aggregate of form.

Similarly, all of the mental states that are pleasurable, painful, and neutral experiences, whether they occur within one's own mind or that of another, are the aggregate of sensation. The apprehension of marks is the aggregate of identification. All formations that are not included in one of the other four aggregates constitute the aggregate of formation, as illustrated by the mental states that bring about the mind's engagement with an object. Consciousness is that which has the nature of the six or eight collections.

THE ELEMENTS

On the second topic, the treatise states:

> **The meanings of the seminal factor**
> **Of the apprehender, apprehended,**
> **And apprehension are held to be different. [III.17c-d]**

The term "element" has three **meanings:** it has the sense **of** being the **seminal factor** of either the apprehended, the apprehender, or of apprehension itself. **The apprehender** refers to the eye element and so forth; the **apprehended** refers to the element of form and the other [sense objects]; **and apprehension** refers to elements of the eye consciousness and so forth. These **are held to be different** from those in the previous section [on the aggregates].

"Element" has the meaning of cause, basis, and seed and can be divided into eighteen components. The six faculties, from the eye to the mind, are identical with the respective six elements. As these six faculties possess the quality of, and capacity for, apprehending their particular objects, they are seminal factors associated with [subjective] apprehension. There can be no seeing or any other type of apprehension independent of these factors.

In a conventional sense, each of these has its own essential nature, like fire and its heat. It is on this basis that they are called "elements." In the same way, that which has the capacity to make a sprout grow can be called the "element" of the seed. Thus, faculties have the capacity to apprehend their objects not only when they are supported [by consciousness], but also when they are not, in the same way that a seed does not lose this particular quality even when kept in a box.

Similarly, the next six elements, from form up to the element of phenomena, have the sense of being the seeds or bases for the subject's apprehension by the mind and a faculty. An object, faculty, and consciousness arise as a group.

The next six elements are consciousness, from that associated with the eye up to that of the mind. The character of these six is such that they cognize and apprehend their respective objects, such as form, as their clear and aware essence allows them to determine the exact nature of an object in a precise way.

When the text says, "...are held to be different," it refers to the mere fact that this field of expertise, the elements, is held to be different from the first topic, which was explained in the previous section. This should be understood to apply to what follows as well.

THE SENSE SOURCES

On the third topic, the treatise states:

> **The gateways that lead to encounters,**
> **Sensation, and object determination are different. [III.18a-b]**

The sense sources are **gateways that lead to encounters** and, hence, consciousness. To elaborate, the inner sense sources are gateways that lead to an encounter that entails **sensation and** the outer sense sources are gateways to an encounter that entails **object determination**. These **are different** from the previous [two topics].

Of the twelve sense sources, the inner six are gateways that lead to the arising, or occurrence, of sensory encounter. This includes the sense source of the eye up to and including that of the mind. Pleasure, pain, and other sensations are experienced when the eye and the other six inner sense sources encounter the nature of the six objects.

The six outer sense sources, from form to phenomena, are gateways to an encounter in which the nature of the individual objects is determined. It is because of the very existence of form and other objects that the encounters involving cognition and determination of these objects can take place.

The sense sources are also said to be the gateway to the arising of cognition. The cognition of objects arises and unfolds via these gateways; hence, the name "sense source."[34] Form and the other [five apprehended sources] are, in this way, objects that are determined. Because the eye and the other faculties are what encounter the sensations that arise from these objects and so forth, cognition arises from the subject and object coming together. The term "encounter" is used to indicate how cognition comes to engage its various [objects]. The twelve sense sources are the gateway to the occurrence of this [encounter and cognition of objects]. They encompass all outer and inner phenomena.

Furthermore, anything that can be designated a "phenomenon" is done so by virtue of its appearing to cognition. All forms of pleasure and pain arise from such [appearances] and have no existence apart from being a mental experience. Thus, cognition itself designates and is the primary factor among all those that are termed "phenomena." This has been taught here via a presentation of the gateways through which cognition arises and unfolds.

DEPENDENT ORIGINATION

On the fourth topic, the treatise states:

> Cause, effect, and effort,
> Without exaggeration and denigration. [III.18c-d]

In essence, dependent origination is **cause, effect, and** productive **effort, without exaggeration and denigration.**

"Dependent origination" refers to the fact that all outer and inner phenomena arise in dependence upon, and in relation to, causes and conditions. The entire inner realm of sentient beings comes about through the twelve links of dependent origination, which run from ignorance through old age and death. All outer phenomena as well arise through the gathering of causes and conditions, just as a sprout arises from a seed. They are not uncaused, nor do they arise from things that are not their causes, such as time or the Almighty.

This knowledge enables one to resolve accurately, without exaggerating or denigrating, what the productive causes and specific effects of phenomena are. It also enables one to resolve what the nature of the efforts, or functions, is when causes produce their effects. This is how one gains expertise regarding the meaning of dependent origination. In this context, exaggeration refers to taking something that is not the cause of a particular result to be its cause, as is the case when sentient beings are believed to be created by time or the Almighty. Denigration, on the other hand, entails denying a cause to be so, as when, for example, it is held that the five aggregates in one's present life did not arise from the five aggregates of a previous life, or when it is believed that karma and the afflictions are not what cause sentient beings to be born.

Exaggeration can also occur with respect to results. It may be asserted, for example, that the universe has resulted from an act of the Almighty, or that it arose by virtue of its own nature. The denigration of results can involve claiming that karma does not ripen, that there are no future lives, or that there is no cessation. In other words, this is the case whenever a result that [actually] exists is denigrated.

When a cause gives rise to a result, certain efforts, or functions, are involved. These too can be exaggerated. For example, when a sprout arises from a seed or a formation comes about due to ignorance, it might be believed that these causes create their effects intentionally, with the particular wish to do so. Similarly, one might believe in an independent creator, such as the Almighty, who is able to will these factors to take on their role as agents. When such functions are denigrated, causes are held to lack the capacity to produce [a result]. For example, one might believe that causes cannot produce any effects because when the effects are present, the causes will have already ceased.

In short, all causes and effects are momentary. What is present in a previous moment no longer exists at a later point in time. At the particular time of a cause, in that one moment, there is nothing else called "effort" or "function" that can bring about an effect. And yet, when its constellation of causes is complete, the effect cannot but arise. Cause and effect are posited simply in consideration of this fact.

The causal moment does not involve any effort, any desire to produce a result. However, this does not mean that the ability to produce a result is lacking. All phenomena come about in the absence of a creator; they occur due to dependent origination. Something like a seed or ignorance does not have the thought "I will create a sprout" or "I will create formations." Nor do sprouts or formations think, "I was created by this factor." And yet, unfailingly, they arise in a dependent and interrelated manner. Because all conditioned phenomena are momentary, and because there is no difference in the way each of these arises, ceases, and functions as a cause and effect, this applies to all phenomena.

Certain designations, such as "creator," may be applied from the perspective of a continuity. Such continua [are noticed] when a person first thinks about things like food, clothing, or a home, and subsequently appears to come to experience them. In reality, however, there is no such creator. The intention to plant seeds in the springtime, thinking that one will be able to eat the crops in the autumn, is an indirect cause for the gathering of causes that bring about a harvest. However, it itself is brought about by other preceding causes. In addition, a harvest cannot arise of its own accord by means of the intention alone; it is the gathering of any number of causes that arise after the intention that in the end brings about a harvest. At the time when the result, the harvest, manifests, all of its causes have ceased.

Hence, there is no substantially established creator of the harvest at all. Since things are made by numerous causal factors, and since those causes are momentary, no creator can ever be observed. One might say, "This person planted that tree," and hold to the idea of a creator. However, from the beginning this is just an imputation, in which the idea of a "creator" [is linked] with the continuity of aggregates, a collection of causal factors that are grouped together as a person. One should understand that all the world's conventions are like this.

FACT AND NON-FACT

On the fifth topic, the treatise states:

> The undesired, the desired, purity,
> Co-occurrence, control,
> Attainment, and behavior
> Are, as the meaning of dependency itself, different. [III.19]

Fact and non-fact can be understood via seven dependencies: (1) The dependency of the undesired concerns **the undesired** consequence of one's own negative actions—going to the lower realms. (2) The dependency of **the desired** refers to the desirable consequence of positive actions—going to pleasurable states. (3) The dependency of **purity** concerns the fact that, unless one eliminates the five obscurations and cultivates the factors of enlightenment, suffering will not come to an end. (4) The dependency of **co-occurrence** concerns the fact that two thus-gone ones or two universal emperors do not occur simultaneously within a single world system. (5) The dependency of **control** concerns [the fact that] women do not, for instance, rule as a universal emperor. (6) The dependency of **attainment** concerns [the fact that] women do not attain buddhahood, neither that which is self-realized nor unsurpassable complete buddhahood. And (7) the dependency of **behavior** relates to the fact that someone whose view is excellent will not kill or engage in other [negative acts]. These **are, as the meaning of dependency itself, different** from the preceding topics. For detailed understanding of this topic, consult the *Sūtra on Numerous Elements*.

Generally, what we call knowing fact from non-fact has an extremely broad relevance. It involves knowing which causes produce which effects and which effects are based on which causes. It entails understanding what is possible and what is not, what is fact and what isn't. Such insight enables one to engage the coarse and subtle aspects of all the positive factors associated with the transcendence of suffering, and also to avoid the coarse and subtle aspects of the negative factors linked with cyclic existence.

In this context, the necessity of knowing fact and non-fact in all their aspects is taught via a presentation of seven dependencies. What are these seven? The dependency of the undesired is when, for example, one does not wish to go to the lower realms, but goes there anyway as a result of the karma accumulated while engaging in negative conduct. The dependency of the desired is exemplified by someone who engages in positive actions and, consequently, is reborn in the higher realms as desired. The dependency of purity is exemplified by the fact that there can be no attainment of purity without training on the path and eliminating the obscurations. The dependency of co-occurrence is, for example, that two Buddhas or universal emperors are not found simultaneously within a single world system. This is due to their having accumulated unrivaled karma. The dependency of control is typified by the fact that with the physical support of a woman's body, one lacks the capacity to take control of the precious wheel and the rest of the seven [possessions of a universal emperor]. The dependency of attainment is exemplified by the fact that one can neither attain the level of a Self-realized Buddha nor buddhahood itself with the physical support of a woman's body. The dependency of behavior is, for example, the fact that a noble being will not kill and so forth.

In this way, the meaning of dependency itself is contained in these seven, which comprise the three dependencies of karma, afflictions, and life. For example, it is a fact that by means of negative karma one will go to the lower realms, while negative karma bringing one to the higher realms is a non-fact, an impossibility. This is called the dependency of the undesired, for although there is no one who wants to go to the lower realms, if the cause of going there is present, in dependence upon having previously accumulated non-virtuous karma, one's desires will not enable one to reverse course. Similarly, it is a fact that virtuous karma will bring one to the higher realms, while it is not a fact that it will result in a rebirth in the lower realms. Hence, the desired attainment of the higher realms also depends upon having previously accumulated virtuous karma and is, thus, a dependency; it is not that one enters the higher realms based on one's own desire. Similarly, eliminating the defilements should be understood to lead to the attainment of complete purity, while not having eliminated them will not.

This applies to the rest as well: When the particular circumstances for their existence are present, things come into being, and when these circumstances are not present, they do not. This illustrates the fact that that the intrinsic nature of a phenomenon is as it is; it cannot be altered by the desires of beings. This understanding should be employed skillfully, enabling one to make practical choices based on knowing what is and is not fact regarding all the various phenomena.

THE FACULTIES

On the sixth topic, the treatise states:

> For apprehension, abidance, continuity,
> Experience, and the two purities. [III.20a-b]

There are twenty-two faculties. For the **apprehension** of form and the rest of the six objects, the eyes and the remainder of the six faculties have control. **Abidance** is controlled by the life-force faculty, while the **continuity** of the family is controlled by the male and female faculties. The **experience** of the effects of virtue and non-virtue is controlled by sensations, **and the two** mundane and supramundane **purities** are controlled, respectively, by the five faculties, faith and so forth, and by the three faculties, total understanding and so on.

As taught to the Brahmin Jātiśrona there are twenty-two faculties: (1-5) the eye and the other sense faculties that have form; (6) the mental faculty, (7) the life faculty, (8-9) the male and female faculties, and (10-14) the five faculties that are the sensations of pleasure, mental pleasure, pain, mental pain, and neutrality; (15-19) the five faculties that include faith; and (20-22) the faculty that brings total understanding of what is not understood, the faculty of total understanding, and the faculty of having gained total understanding.

Of these, the "faculty that brings total understanding" refers to nine faculties that are present in the mind stream of those on the path of seeing: the mental faculty, the five faculties that include faith and the faculties of pleasurable sensation, mental pleasure, and neutrality. Similarly, when these nine are present in the mind stream of one on the path of cultivation, they are called the "faculty of total understanding," and they are called the "faculty of having gained total understanding" when they are present in the mind stream of one on the path beyond training.

What do these faculties control? The six faculties, from the eye to the mental faculty, control the apprehension of their own objects, form and so forth. The life-force faculty governs one's abiding as a member of a particular class [of sentient beings]. The male and female faculties control the continuity of womb birth. Pleasure and the rest of the five faculties that are sensations govern the experience of the results that ensue from virtue and non-virtue. The five faculties that include faith and the three that include that which brings total understanding control the two types of purity. How so? The five faculties that include faith control mundane purity, while the three faculties that include that which brings total understanding control supramundane purity. These twenty-two are termed "faculties" with reference to the governing role they play.

TIME

On the seventh topic, the treatise states:

> **Effect and cause having been experienced**
> **And not experienced are different. [III.20c-d]**

Time is explained as follows: The past is **effect and cause having** already **been experienced**, while the present refers to the cause having been experienced, but not the effect, **and** the future is when these two have **not** yet been **experienced**. Again, these **are different** from the topics taught previously.

That which we call "time" is designated in consideration of the arising and ceasing of a given entity. Entities do have causes, and whenever a resultant phenomenon has already been experienced it is "the past." Having already been experienced and established, it has now ceased. If an experience of the result has already occurred, its cause should also implicitly be understood to have ceased. Thus, an entity that was once established by its causes but is no longer existent is referred to as "the past."

When certain causes have already been experienced, but the experience of the result is not over, it is called "the present." The assembly of causes being complete and then ceasing provides the impetus for the present existence of a result. It does not make sense for a cause to exist when its result is present. Hence, we speak of "the present" from the point of view of a result that has not yet ceased.

Similarly, when neither the cause nor result have been experienced or become manifest, the term "future" is used. Although the causes associated with the manifestation of a resultant phenomenon may be present in the future, if at present their assembly is incomplete and they do not have the unobstructed ability to function as its direct cause, then it is said that "the cause has not yet been experienced." If the causes had already been experienced, their result would need to be present right away. Furthermore, it goes without saying that as long as these causes have not been experienced, their result cannot be experienced either.

This approach can be used to understand the three times, regardless of whether we are speaking in terms of subtle moments or applying the convention of the three times to coarse continua. In this way, what we refer to as "time" is composed of three aspects, which can be applied to the shortest moments of time all the way up to great eons. Though the factor of time is [actually] a string of moments, many such moments may be grouped together and labeled in various ways, such as "the present eon." Hence, it should be understood that this process of using conventions allows us to make various classifications.

THE TRUTHS

On the eighth topic, the treatise states:

> With a meaning that entails sensation and its cause,
> The establishment of the cause of this,
> The pacification of these, and the remedy—
> This is held to be different. [III.21]

The truths are explained as follows: The truth of suffering is endowed with a meaning that entails defiling sensation and its cause. The truth of the origin refers to the establishment of the cause of this suffering, karma, and affliction. The truth of cessation is the pacification of these two. And the truth of the path is the remedy. This is held to be different from the topics taught above.

"The truth" is [here] a meaning which is seen to be true and undeceiving from the perspective of a noble being who perceives the intrinsic nature of an entity as it really is. When divided in terms of the causes and effects of affliction and purification, there are four truths. What are they? Those properties that are comprised of defiling sensations that possess any of the three types of suffering together with their cause or basis, the five aggregates, are the truth of suffering. The cause of this suffering is that which functions as the source for, or that which establishes, the repeated births of cyclic existence. This refers to karma and affliction; it is these that are termed "the truth of the origin." The permanent pacification of suffering and its origin is "the truth of cessation," while "the truth of the path" is understood to be a remedy that brings about the exhaustion of all defiling phenomena. In other words, the truth of the path is the knowledge associated with the realization of selflessness, along with its subsidiary factors.

THE VEHICLES

On the ninth topic, the treatise states:

> Understanding the qualities and flaws, and non-conceptuality,
> Brings a definitive emergence by relying on others
> And by oneself—hence, this is different. [III.22a-c]

The explanation of the three vehicles is as follows: The Listeners and Self-realized Buddhas have an understanding of the distinct qualities of the transcendence of suffering and the flaws of cyclic existence, and in the vehicle of the Bodhisattvas, the meaning of **non-conceptuality** is understood. This understanding **brings a definitive emergence.** In the case of the Listeners, these qualities and flaws are understood **by relying on others,** i.e., by learning from them, while the Self-realized Buddhas attain their definitive emergence on their own. **And** in the vehicle of the Bodhisattvas, definitive emergence is attained **by oneself** via non-conceptual wakefulness. **Hence, this** topic **is different** from those taught above.

The term "vehicle" is based on the [Sanskrit] word *yāna,* which can mean various things, including "carriage." It is used to show that on a given path, the person who enters or rides such a vehicle will be carried towards, and delivered to, their desired fruition. In that regard, the term "causal vehicle" refers to that which is a means for traveling the path to the fruition, whereas the "resultant vehicle" refers to that within which the journey takes place by means of the very fruition that is to be attained. Such vehicles can be classified in various ways by considering their status as either mundane or supramundane. Nevertheless, in this context the explanation concerns the three Vehicles of Liberation, those of the Listeners, the Self-realized Buddhas, and the Bodhisattvas. These three can be further condensed into two categories: the Great Vehicle and the Lesser Vehicle.

The differences between these are explained in the following way: The "Vehicle of the Listeners" is referred to as such because one "listens" to an external master, learning about the positive qualities of the transcendence of suffering and the flaws of cyclic existence. In understanding the nature of these two, one emerges definitively from and pacifies the suffering of cyclic existence. This is the specific result of this vehicle. In the "Vehicle of the Self-realized Buddhas," in contrast, one fully understands these qualities and flaws on one's own, without depending on a master, which allows one to emerge definitively at the level of peace.

In the "Great Vehicle" one does not form the idea that the flaws and qualities of cyclic existence and transcendence of suffering are different from one another. Instead, they are understood to be fundamentally the same. With this understanding, one emerges definitively so as to attain the great transcendence of suffering, confined neither to existence nor to peace. It is also taught that one should be aware of the fact that this achievement is due to two factors: the outer master, a spiritual friend other than oneself, and the inner master, the unity of profound knowledge and means within one's own mind stream.

THE CONDITIONED AND UNCONDITIONED

On the tenth topic, the treatise states:

> The reasons along with their designations and cause,
> Complete pacification and its object—
> Thus is the last explained. [III.22d-f]

These stanzas on reality constitute the third chapter of the treatise *Distinguishing the Middle from Extremes.*

The conditioned is explained to be **the reasons**, those subsumed under place, body, and sense objects, **along with their designations** (by combinations of words and the like) **and cause** (the all-ground consciousness that is composed of seeds). The unconditioned, in contrast, is explained to be **complete pacification**, cessation, **and its object**, suchness. **Thus is the last** topic **explained.**

The summation of the meaning of reality contains two categories: mirror-like reality and apparent reality. Mirror-like reality is the fundamental reality, while the remaining [types of reality] are what appear within it. These nine types of apparent reality are as follows: (1) the apparent reality free from pride; (2) the apparent reality that remedies the mistaken; (3) the apparent reality of the Vehicle of the Listeners' definitive emergence; (4) the apparent reality of the Great Vehicle's definitive emergence, which matures through the coarse and liberates through the subtle; (5) the apparent reality of the elimination of opponents using reasoning supported by examples; (6) the apparent reality of the full expression of the Great Vehicle; (7) the apparent reality of engaging all objects of cognition; (8) the apparent reality of the full expression of the unmistaken suchness; and (9) the apparent reality of the realization of all intents regarding the basis for the apprehension of the self.

[The conditioned] is explained to be all relative phenomena: that which is designated by means of names, sentences, or syllables and which is caused. The cause [of conditioned phenomena] is the all-ground consciousness itself, because it is from this element, the accumulation of various habitual tendencies, that all appearances arise.

The phrase "The reasons along with…" refers to outer and inner appearances. These appearances are the bases or reasons for giving names. What are they? That which appears as outer objects includes (1) appearances of place (i.e., the appearance of things like mountains and continents of the vessel-like world), (2) appearances of body (the individual bodies of sentient beings), and (3) appearances of sense objects (such as form). That which appears as an inner apprehender comprises the seven collections of consciousness. These are the defiled mental consciousness, the five collections of [sense] consciousness, and the mental consciousness, which is also known as "conception." In this way, all outer and inner appearances are aspects of the all-ground consciousness's ripening. They are referred to as "conditioned phenomena" because they are impermanent and conditioned by their causes, karma and affliction.

The "unconditioned," in contrast, refers to the complete pacification of cessation, as well as to its object. The latter refers to suchness, the focal point of the path. The path is the subjective side of suchness and is that which brings about pacification. As such, there is nothing wrong with considering it an aspect of pacification. Neither is there any problem with terming it "unconditioned," since it is not conditioned by karma and the afflictions. Nevertheless, the essence of the path is such that it arises and ceases. Thus, it is not unconditioned in a genuine sense. Gaining expertise regarding the conditioned and unconditioned is explained to be the last of the ten fields of expertise.

Explained in this way, suchness, referred to by the words "and its object," and the complete pacification of cessation can be included as aspects of the fruition, the path beyond training. Thus, when [it is taught that] all objects of cognition are included within the five categories, an additional distinction may be drawn between conditioned and unconditioned phenomena. Such an explanatory approach is attractive in general, and particularly so in the context of the Mind Only system.

From a general perspective, the conditioned can be distinguished as reasons that are described and caused. These are the bases for the imaginary and the product of the dependent nature. In other words, it includes everything that is causally produced, everything that arises and ceases. The nature of the complete pacification of all designations and all that arises and ceases based on causes and conditions is not a complete nonexistence, as is the case with the horns of a rabbit. It is, rather, thoroughly established suchness, the unconditioned. Such an exposition, I believe, does not contain any actual problems.

This was the commentary to the third chapter of the treatise *Distinguishing the Middle from Extremes*, the stanzas on reality.

FOUR
THE PATH OF PRACTICE

The second topic is the path of practice. This section concerns (1) the features of the path, (2) the phases of the path, and (3) the results of the path.

FEATURES OF THE PATH

The first of these involves (1) a presentation of the thirty-seven factors of enlightenment and their relationship to the five paths, (2) a division of these factors into three phases, and (3) an explanation of the distinguishing features of the Bodhisattva's path.

THE THIRTY-SEVEN FACTORS OF ENLIGHTENMENT

The first topic includes explanations of (1) the four applications of mindfulness that occur on the lesser path of accumulation; (2) the four authentic eliminations that occur on the intermediate path of accumulation; (3) the four bases of miraculous power that occur on the greater path of accumulation; (4) the five faculties that occur on the first two stages of the path of joining, the stages of heat and summit; (5) the five powers that occur on the last two stages of the path of joining, the stages of acceptance and supreme quality; (6) the seven aspects of enlightenment that occur on the path of seeing; and (7) the eightfold noble path that occurs on the path of cultivation.

THE FOUR APPLICATIONS OF MINDFULNESS

On the first topic, the treatise states:

By negative tendencies, the cause of craving,
The basis, and no delusion—
The applications of mindfulness
Are cultivated to access the four truths. [IV.1]

The cultivation of remedies refers to the cultivation of the factors of enlightenment. Of these, the applications of mindfulness are presented first. (1) **By** investigating the body, which makes the **negative tendencies** fully evident, the truth of suffering can be accessed. (2) By thoroughly analyzing sensation, **the** main **cause of craving**, the truth of origin can be accessed. (3) By investigating the mind, **the basis** for the apprehension of the self, the truth of cessation can be accessed. (4) **And,** by thoroughly analyzing phenomena, there is **no delusion** about the thoroughly afflicted and completely purified. Through this, the truth of the path is accessed. Thus, **the applications of mindfulness are cultivated to access the four truths.**

The body is the basis for "negative tendencies," insofar as this term refers to defiling formations. By being mindful of the body's nature, which is the ripening of suffering, the truth of suffering can be accessed. Sensation is the cause of craving, the main factor involved in the origin of suffering. Therefore, thoroughly investigating sensation enables the truth of origin to be accessed. The ultimate basis for the view of the self is the mind. Investigating it allows the truth of cessation to be accessed. In other words, by comprehending the facts of selflessness and mere awareness, cessation can be accessed without any fear of the self being exterminated. By examining all phenomena, one becomes free of delusion regarding those that are thoroughly afflictive and those that are completely purificatory, and so accesses the truth of the path. In this way, training in the four applications of mindfulness is presented first so that one may access the four noble truths.

The Four Authentic Eliminations

On the second topic, the treatise states:

Once the conflicting factors and their remedies
Are perfectly understood in every way,

Four types of diligence arise
That are directed towards eliminating these. [IV.2]

The authentic eliminations are taught next. **Once the conflicting factors and their remedies are perfectly understood in every way,** which is brought about by cultivating the applications of mindfulness as shown above, **four types of diligence arise that are directed towards eliminating these** conflicting factors and cultivating their remedies. Individually, these are (1) preventing the arising of conflicting factors that have not yet occurred; (2) eliminating those that have occurred; (3) producing remedies that have not occurred; and (4) developing those that have.

By training in the four applications of mindfulness in the manner described above, the conflicting factors that are eliminated and the remedies that effect this elimination will be perfectly understood in every way. Once this occurs, four types of diligence will arise that are directed towards the elimination of conflicting factors: (1) striving to eliminate non-virtuous factors that have already occurred, (2) striving to prevent non-virtuous factors that have not yet occurred from arising, (3) striving to produce virtuous factors that have not yet occurred, and (4) striving to prevent virtuous factors that have already occurred from deteriorating.

THE FOUR BASES OF MIRACULOUS POWER

The third topic, the explanation of the four bases of miraculous power, includes (1) a brief presentation of the purpose of the four bases of miraculous power and the way in which they are produced, and (2) a detailed explanation of their nature.

DEVELOPING THE FOUR BASES OF MIRACULOUS POWER

On the first topic, the treatise states:

Focus and flexibility
Enable one to accomplish every goal.
This comes about in reliance on its cause,
The eight applications that eliminate the five flaws. [IV.3]

As one practices diligently to eliminate these factors, the mind remains focused and achieves flexibility. Consequently, one develops the four bases of miraculous power, which are causes that enable one to accomplish every goal. These four meditative absorptions are distinguished with reference to the factors that assist them—intention, diligence, volition, and discernment. In this way, the bases of miraculous power follow the authentic eliminations. This flexibility comes about in reliance on its cause, the eight applications that eliminate the five flaws.

By cultivating diligence in the manner described above, the mind will be able to remain in a state of one-pointed concentration and become extremely flexible. This allows one to accomplish the various types of super-knowledge, as well as every other goal. Meditative absorptions that possess this type of mental flexibility arise in dependence upon a specific cause, the eight applications that eliminate the five flaws.

DETAILED EXPLANATION

The second section presents (1) the five flaws that are eliminated, and (2) how to apply their remedy, the eight applications.

THE FIVE FLAWS

On the first topic, the treatise states:

> Being lazy, forgetting the instructions,
> Dullness and agitation,
> Non-application, and application—
> These are held to be the five flaws. [IV.4]

What are the five flaws? They are (1) **being lazy** when it comes to the cultivation of meditative absorption; (2) **forgetting the instructions** on how to meditate; (3) **dullness and agitation**, which are counted as one flaw; (4) **non-application**, when it comes to pacifying these two; and (5) over-**application** once they have already been thoroughly pacified—these are held to be the five flaws.

What are the five flaws that hinder the accomplishment of meditative absorption? They are (1) falling under the sway of laziness and, consequently, not exerting oneself, and (2) forgetting the instructions on meditative absorption; both of these hinder taking up the practice of meditative absorption. (3) Dullness and agitation hinder the actual practice of meditative absorption; the former is a state of inner withdrawal and the latter a proliferation of thought activity directed towards external objects. These two are counted as a single flaw. (4) When one is engaged in meditative absorption and dullness, agitation, or another flaw occurs, one should apply the appropriate remedy. Not applying the remedy in such a way is a hindrance. (5) On the other hand, once the remedies have been used to pacify dullness and agitation, to go on applying them in an excessive manner is also a hindrance, because that itself is a factor that creates turbulence. These last two flaws keep one's meditative absorption from developing. Laziness and the other four factors presented here are asserted to be the five flaws.

THE EIGHT APPLICATIONS

On the second topic, the treatise states:

> **The basis and what is based on this,**
> **Cause and result,**
> **To not forget one's focal point and**
> **To notice dullness or agitation,**
> **To fully apply oneself to the elimination of these factors**
> **And rest naturally once pacified. [IV.5]**

The eight applications that eliminate these flaws are classified as follows. (1) Intention, **the basis** for effort, and (2) effort, **what is based on this** intention; (3) faith, the **cause,** or basis, of intention; **and** (4) flexibility, the **result** that rests on [the basis of] effort. The four remaining applications that eliminate [their respective flaws] are as follows: (5) mindfulness, **to not forget one's focal point and** (6) alertness, **to notice** the presence of either **dullness or agitation;** (7) volition, which allows one **to fully apply oneself to the elimination of these factors** once they have been noticed; **and** (8) equanimity, the mind's **resting naturally once** dullness and agitation have been **pacified.**

There are four remedies that lead to the elimination of laziness: faith, intention, effort, and flexibility. If flexibility is attained laziness will not occur. This flexibility, in turn, is achieved through effort, which is itself attained by having one's intent directed towards cultivating meditative absorption. Intention arises by having trust and faith in this [practice] at the outset. Therefore, effort is based on intention, the explicit desire to achieve meditative absorption, while intention forms the basis for effort. The cause of this intention is faith and the result of effort is the achievement of flexibility. Laziness is eliminated by means of these four remedies.

Similarly, there are four remedies associated with the remaining four flaws: mindfulness, alertness, volition, and equanimity. Mindfulness prevents one from forgetting the focal point of the instructions. Alertness notices and comprehends occurrences of dullness and agitation. Volition allows one to apply the remedies that eliminate the flaws of dullness and agitation, while equanimity settles the mind in a natural state of ease once they have been pacified.

THE FIVE FACULTIES

On the fourth topic, the treatise states:

> When the factors conducive to liberation have been developed,
> There is control over intention and application,
> The focal point is not forgotten,
> Discursiveness does not occur, and discernment is present.
> [IV.6]

What follows are the five faculties. **When** the four bases of miraculous power have made the mind flexible and **the** fundamental virtues that are **factors conducive to liberation have been developed, there is control over** [four factors]: (1) Faith leads to control over **intention** concerning the acceptance and rejection of the four truths, **and** (2) diligence brings control over the **application** of this [acceptance and rejection]. (3) Mindfulness leads to a control in which **the focal point is not forgotten;** (4) meditative absorption brings control over the mind, ensuring that **discursiveness does not occur; and** (5) knowledge allows for a control such that **discernment is present.**

Once the four bases of miraculous power have made the mind flexible and the fundamental virtues that are factors conducive to liberation have been developed, one gains control [over four things]. Faith leads to control over intention concerning the acceptance and rejection of the four truths, while diligence brings control over application, i.e., putting [this intention] into practice. The word "control" that appears in the middle of this stanza is a so-called interspersed clarifier. It should be understood to apply throughout, to each of the remaining three faculties. Mindfulness brings a control that keeps one from forgetting one's focal point, meditative absorption keeps the proliferation of irrelevant thoughts at bay, and knowledge allows for the discernment of phenomena. In this way, the five faculties usher in the qualities of complete purity.

THE FIVE POWERS

The fifth topic explains the five powers. This section includes (1) the actual [presentation of the five powers], and (2) a summation demonstrating how the powers are linked with the path of joining.

THE ACTUAL PRESENTATION

On the first division, the treatise states:

> **Because the factors that conflict with them are weakened,**
> **They become powers. The latter are effects. [IV.7a-b]**

Once faith and the other faculties have gained strength, they are referred to as "powers." Thus, **because the factors that conflict with them are weakened, they become powers.** What is the reason for presenting faith and the rest in this particular sequence? **The latter are** the effects of the former. Thus, due to faith one musters diligence. By being diligent one will come to be mindful. Being mindful will allow one to rest in equanimity. And by resting in equanimity one will come to the understanding of reality as it actually is.

Faith and the rest of the five faculties become powerful because the factors that conflict with them—lack of faith, laziness, forgetfulness, distraction, and bewilderment or distorted knowledge—are diminished and weakened. They are referred to as "powers," such as the "power of faith," because they cannot be overcome by the factors that conflict with them. Furthermore, of these faculties and powers, the latter are effects of the former. Faith causes diligence, which in turn causes mindfulness. From mindfulness arises meditative absorption, the ability to rest in equanimity, which eventually results in knowledge of reality as it actually is.

SUMMARY

On the second topic, the treatise states:

> For both the faculties and the powers
> There are two factors conducive to ascertainment. [IV.7c-d]

> **For both the faculties and the powers there are two** [sets of] **factors conducive to ascertainment.** These two are [the phases of] heat and summit, which are when the faculties occur, and [the phases of] acceptance and supreme property associated with the powers.

The phases of the five faculties and the five powers are factors conducive to ascertainment. These factors are posited with reference to the first two and latter two of the four stages of the path of joining. How so? The five faculties should be understood to be present on the two stages of heat and summit and the five powers on the two stages of acceptance and supreme property.

THE SEVEN ASPECTS OF ENLIGHTENMENT

On the sixth topic, the treatise states:

> The aspect of nature, the aspect of basis,
> The third aspect of definitive emergence,
> And the fourth aspect of benefit;
> The three aspects of freedom from affliction [IV.8]

> Are taught to be the foundation, state,
> And the essential nature. [IV.9a-b]

The seven aspects of enlightenment come next on the path of seeing. How are these classified? Fully discerning phenomena is **the aspect of nature** and mindfulness is **the enlightenment aspect of basis.** Diligence is **the third aspect of definitive emergence** and joy is **the fourth aspect,** that of benefit. The three aspects of freedom from thorough affliction are agility, meditative absorption, and equanimity. Of these, agility is taught to be the foundation for absence of thorough affliction because it is the remedy for negative tendencies. Meditative absorption is the state in which thorough affliction is absent and equanimity is the essential nature of absence of affliction.

The seven aspects of enlightenment are mindfulness, fully discerning phenomena, diligence, joy, agility, meditative absorption, and equanimity. The knowledge that fully discerns phenomena is referred to as the aspect of nature, owing to the fact that the knowledge that perceives the truth of the intrinsic nature is the essence of the path of seeing. Therefore, it is referred to as the essence, or nature, of enlightenment. Mindfulness is the aspect of the basis of enlightenment because it is the basis of good qualities. Diligence is the aspect of definitive emergence because it allows one to transcend the conflicting factors. Joy is the aspect of benefit, the desirable quality that is obtained by [practicing] the paths. Agility, meditative absorption, and equanimity are aspects that are free from affliction. To elaborate, agility is taught to be the foundation for freedom from affliction; meditative absorption, the state of freedom from affliction; and equanimity, the essential nature of freedom from affliction.

THE EIGHTFOLD NOBLE PATH

On the seventh topic, the treatise states:

Determination, production of understanding,
Three aspects that instill confidence in others, [IV.9c-d]

And the remedy for conflicting factors—
These are the eight aspects of the path.
It is held that others are made aware of
The view, discipline, and few material needs. [IV.10]

Afflictions, subsidiary afflictions, and mastery—
These remedy the conflicting factors. [IV.11a-b]

Next, there are eight aspects of the path that occur on the path of cultivation. Authentic view is the aspect that provides determination. It is a mundane factor that is obtained subsequent to the supramundane and which determines one's own realization. Authentic thought and authentic speech are aspects that bring about an understanding in others; the **production of understanding** is brought about by intentional speech. Authentic speech, activity, and livelihood are **three aspects that instill confidence in others, and** authentic effort, mindfulness, and meditative absorption constitute **the remedy for conflicting factors. These are the eight aspects of the path.**

Moreover, **it is held that others are made aware of the view, discipline, and** [the benefits of having] **few material needs** via, respectively, authentic speech, activity, and livelihood. Authentic effort functions as a remedy against the **afflictions** that are eliminated on the path of cultivation. Authentic mindfulness allows one to remain perfectly mindful of the reasons for calm abiding and so forth. Since it ensures the absence of dullness and agitation, it acts as a remedy against the **subsidiary afflictions.** In authentic meditative absorption, one rests in a state of concentration. This functions as a remedy for the factors that inhibit equilibrium **and** prevent **mastery** of the super-knowledges and other extraordinary qualities. Hence, **these remedy the conflicting factors.**

The eightfold noble path is taught to include authentic view, thought, speech, activity, livelihood, effort, mindfulness, and meditative absorption. The nature of the authentic view is such that it determines the way objects really are. As the stainless knowledge that is attained subsequent to the direct perception of the intrinsic nature on the path of seeing, it manifests as a certainty that apprehends, or determines, the significance of the reality realized [in meditative equipoise]. Authentic thought and authentic speech elicit understanding in others. Authentic thought is the motivation to teach others exactly what oneself has understood. To speak with such motivation is authentic speech. Both possess a stainless authenticity.

Authentic speech, activity, and livelihood are the three aspects that instill confidence in others. How so? It is held that authentic speech makes others aware of the [speaker's] pure view and so instills confidence in them. Authentic activity is the complete non-engagement in all that is evil and unvirtuous; it is discipline that pleases the noble ones, attained by power of the intrinsic nature. Through such activity, others are made aware of pure discipline. This instills confidence in them. Authentic livelihood is a noble being's complete disengagement from wrong livelihood, that which is based on flattery and so forth. Authentic livelihood makes others aware that [the noble one] has few material needs. This too instills confidence.

Effort, meditative absorption, and mindfulness remedy the factors that conflict with the path. Effort eliminates those afflictions that are discarded via the path of cultivation. Mindfulness eliminates the subsidiary afflictions of dullness and agitation because it allows [the mind] to focus intensely on the causes for calm abiding and so forth. Because the super-knowledges and other qualities are accomplished by abiding in meditative concentration, meditative absorption remedies the factors that conflict with the mastery of such extraordinary qualities. Thus, view and the remaining seven aspects are the eight aspects that constitute the path of the noble ones.

THE THREE PHASES

On the second topic, the treatise states:

> In accord, yet mistaken;
> Related, but opposed; [IV.11c-d]
>
> Unmistaken and unrelated to error—
> These are the cultivations. [IV.12a-b]

In short, these remedies can be cultivated in three ways: (1) The cultivation that occurs on the paths of accumulation and joining is **in accord** with the unmistaken, **yet** still **mistaken.** (2) The cultivation of noble ones who are training is **related** to the errors that are eliminated via cultivation, **but** in essence, **opposed** to them. (3) The cultivation beyond training is essentially **unmistaken and unrelated to error—these are the cultivations.**

All of the five paths are contained within three phases. On the paths of accumulation and joining, the path is cultivated by means of the four applications of mindfulness and so forth. These are unmistaken in the sense that the understanding one cultivates through study and reflection accords with reality. However, they are also instances of being mistaken because one conceives of the object universal of the absence of the self as if it were the specific characteristics that pertain to the absence of self.[35] In the context of the paths of seeing and cultivation, there is still a connection with errors that obscure. Nevertheless, since the meaning of selflessness is perceived directly, they are opposed to error. On the path beyond training the path has already been completed; the essence of the intrinsic nature is seen directly and all obscurations, including their habitual tendencies, have been eliminated. For this reason, here cultivation is unrelated to error.

WHAT DISTINGUISHES THE BODHISATTVA PATH

On the third topic, the treatise states:

> In the case of the Bodhisattvas,[36]
> Focus, directing the mind,
> And attainment are superior. [IV.12c-d]

The Listeners and Self-realized Buddhas focus only on the body and the other factors included in their own stream of being. **In the case of the Bodhisattvas,** however, the **focus** encompasses everything, that which is included in their own stream of being, as well as that of others. The Listeners and Self-realized Buddhas direct their minds to the body and [the other foundations for mindfulness] as being impermanent and so forth. For the Bodhisattvas, in contrast, **directing the mind** does not involve focusing on anything. The Listeners and Self-realized Buddhas train to separate from the body and the other [aggregates] at all costs. The Bodhisattvas do not train to separate from the body, nor to do the opposite. Instead, they train to attain the non-abiding transcendence of suffering. **And** thus, their **attainment**s as well **are superior.**

When Bodhisattvas train on the path using the four applications of mindfulness and so forth, there are three distinct qualities that make their path superior. What are they? (1) Their focus is vast. The Bodhisattvas focus on the entire range of phenomena contained within their own stream of being and that of others. In doing so, they view the nature of these phenomena as devoid of the two kinds of self. The focus of the Listeners and Self-realized Buddhas is narrow in comparison. In focusing primarily on the phenomena in their own streams of being, they observe only the absence of the personal self. (2) They direct their minds in a way that is beyond focus. The Listeners and Self-realized Buddhas direct their minds to the marks of impermanence and so forth. The Bodhisattvas, in contrast, direct their minds in a way that is free from all exaggeration and denigration, free from [believing in] permanence, impermanence, and so forth. (3) They attain the non-abiding transcendence of suffering. The Listeners and Self-realized Buddhas [seek to] part with factors like the impure body. Consequently, they attain a lesser transcendence of suffering. The Bodhisattvas, however, do not practice to either separate or not separate from factors such as the body. Instead, they practice to attain the non-abiding transcendence of suffering. The practice of the Bodhisattvas is superior in these three ways.

PHASES OF THE PATH

Second, the phases of the path are presented in two ways: (1) as nine phases, and (2) as three phases.

NINE PHASES

The first of these divisions involves a discussion of (1) the actual phases, and (2) how they are classified.

THE ACTUAL PHASES

On the first topic, the treatise states:

> Causal, entry,
> Preparation, so-called result,
> Action, non-action, distinction,
> The superior, and the unsurpassable, [IV.13]

What states are associated with cultivating the remedies? The **causal** state is when an individual has the potential [to practice one of the three vehicles]. The state of **entry** is when one gives rise to the enlightened mind. The state of **preparation** begins with the manifestation of the enlightened mind and continues until the fruition has been attained. The **so-called result**ant state is the attainment of this fruition. The state that involves **action** is the stage of training, while the state of **non-action** is the stage beyond training. The state of **distinction** is when one possesses the super-knowledges and other such special qualities. **The superior** state is that of the Bodhisattva **and the unsurpassable** state is that of perfect buddhahood.

The path is explained to involve nine different phases: (1) The causal state refers to a person who has the potential [to practice one of the vehicles]. (2) The state of entry is when, in the manner of any one of the three vehicles, one gives rise to the enlightened mind. (3) Preparation begins when the enlightened mind has been developed and ends when the first ground is attained. (4) The so-called fruition is the attainment of the first ground. (5) The second ground up to and including the seventh are states that involve activity, concerted effort on the path. (6) The effortless state, the state of non-training, is the eighth ground. (7) The ninth ground is the state in which one possesses distinct qualities, such as correct discrimination and the various types of super-knowledge. (8) The superior ground of training is the tenth. (9) The unsurpassable state is the path beyond training, the ground of buddhahood.

The Classification of These Phases

On the second topic, the treatise states:

> **These are taught to be**
> **Inspiration, engagement,**
> **Definitive emergence, prophecy,**
> **Expression, empowerment,** [IV.14]
>
> **Arrival, benefits, and active accomplishment.** [IV.15a]

These [states] **are taught to be** as follows: The state of **inspiration** is taught to include all grounds of the Bodhisattva's inspired conduct and the state of **engagement,** the first ground. The state of **definitive emergence** is taught to include the next six grounds, the state of **prophecy,** the eighth ground, and the state of **expression,** the ninth ground. The state of **empowerment** is the tenth ground. The state of **arrival** refers to the body of qualities, while the state of **benefits** is the body of perfect enjoyment **and** the state of **active accomplishment** is taught to be the emanation body.

What follows is an additional way of classifying the nine states, different from the one explained above: (1) The paths of accumulation and joining are referred to as the "phase of inspired conduct." This includes the states of potential, entry, and preparation. (2) The first ground is when one has actually set out on the transcendent path. (3) The second to the seventh grounds are states of definitive emergence, in which one actively strives to eliminate [the discards]. (4) On the eighth ground, prophecy is obtained. (5) On the ninth ground, the Dharma is expressed to disciples via the fourfold correct discrimination. (6) On the tenth ground, one is empowered with the great rays of light. (7) The body of qualities is the arrival at the ground of buddhahood, while (8) possessing great benefit is the body of perfect enjoyment, and (9) accomplishing activities for the welfare of disciples is the emanation body. Thus, the nine phases are also taught to be classified in this way.

THREE PHASES

On the third topic, the treatise states:

> The basic field of phenomena has three aspects:
> The impure, impure and pure,
> And the perfectly pure. [IV.15b-d]
>
> It is held that individuals
> Can be appropriately classified through these. [IV.16a-b]

The basic field of phenomena has three aspects. **The impure** state begins with the causal state and continues throughout the state of preparation. The state that is both **impure and pure** is the path of training, **and the perfectly pure** state refers to the path beyond training. **It is held that individuals can be appropriately classified** as, for instance, "one with potential" or "one who has entered," **through these** divisions of the states.

Individuals who are present to the basic field of phenomena go through three phases: (1) The "phase of sentient beings" refers to the period in which impurities have not been purified. (2) The "phase of the Bodhisattva" is when some of the obscurations have been purified, but

not all of them. (3) The stage at which they have all been completely purified is the "phase of buddhahood."

These conventions are applied in a precise way from the perspective
of how things appear. How so? It is held that three types of persons,
or three phases, can be set forth based on the two sets of nine phases
explained above. To elaborate, being at the "causal phase," as well as
those of "entry," "preparation," and "inspiration," is the phase of being an impure sentient being. The phase that is both pure and impure
is comprised of the five phases that start with "result" and end with
"the superior" and the five that begin with "engagement" and proceed
through "empowerment." These are all included in the grounds of the
Bodhisattvas. The four remaining phases, the "unsurpassable," and also
"arrival," "benefits," and "active accomplishment," comprise the phase
of complete purity. These four are within the ground of buddhahood,
the path beyond training.

Vasubandhu explains what is referred to here as "non-action" using
the term "beyond training." He also states that "the superior" refers to
"Bodhisattvas who have entered the grounds superior to those of the
Listeners and so forth." When expounding on Vasubandhu's commentary, Sthiramati interprets the former to mean the [path] beyond training,
the ground of buddhahood. The latter he associates with those who, in
completely realizing both types of selflessness, are superior to the Listeners
and so forth and abide on the grounds of the Great Vehicle's noble ones.
Thus, in his reading, "the unsurpassable" applies to the ground of buddhahood and "the superior" to all [of the ten grounds], rather than to the
tenth ground [alone].

This poses some difficulties, however, because with this reading there is
no specific explanation of two phases, the tenth and the eighth grounds,
while the explanations of that which is "beyond training" and "the unsurpassable" become repetitious. The individual divisions of the two sets of
nine phases cannot be linked with one another in order and, furthermore,
[the explanation of] the phase associated with having entered the grounds
ends up being a repetition of what was already taught.

Therefore, I suggest that the phrase "beyond training" in Vasubandhu's
commentary be taken to refer to the transcendence of efforts that occurs
when training on the path, not to the ground of buddhahood. Likewise,
the reference to those who abide on noble grounds above those of the
Listeners and the Self-realized Buddhas could be understood to refer to
those on the tenth ground, those who are above not only the Listeners,

Self-realized Buddhas, and so forth, but also superior to Bodhisattvas who are training on the nine grounds below.

Not only are there are no problems with such an interpretation, it also contains clear points for properly understanding the structure of the two enumerations and the relationship between them. It appears, however, that I am the only one to have proposed such a reading. I therefore request intelligent individuals to examine this further.

RESULTS OF THE PATH

The third topic involves (1) a general presentation of the five results, and (2) a detailed explanation from the perspective of the path.

THE FIVE RESULTS

On the first topic, the treatise states:

> Becoming a vessel, which is taught to be ripening;
> Strength that ensues from that; [IV.16c-d]

> Desiring, development, and purity—
> This is the sequence of fruition. [IV.17a-b]

What results are attained? There are five: (1) **Becoming a vessel, which is taught to be ripening** that accords with virtue; (2) **strength,** the prevalence of virtue **that ensues from that** (i.e., having become a vessel); (3) **desiring** virtue, which is due to having familiarized oneself with virtue in the past; (4) the **development** of virtue that comes from familiarizing oneself with virtue in the present, **and (5) purity,** the elimination of obscurations. **This is the sequence of** the five **fruitions.**

In general, all fruitions of the path can be grouped into five categories: (1) As a result of practicing virtue, one will attain a [physical] support that makes one a vessel for virtue in all of one's lives. This is explained to be the "ripened result." One who is a vessel for virtue has gained an excellent physical support free from the eight states that lack freedom.[37] When the mind applies itself to virtue, it functions as a vessel or medium that enables virtuous qualities to arise. This is the "ripened result" of virtue that has been engendered in the past. (2) Once one has already become a vessel, possessing the strength to practice purification is the "predominant effect." (3) Wanting to practice virtue again and again is the "effect that accords with its cause." (4) The unprecedented increase and flourishing of virtue in this lifetime by the power of prior habituation to virtue is the "effect of individual effort." (5) The purification of conflicting factors is the "effect of separation." The effects explained here are the fruitions of the path. They are sequential because the latter develop from the former.

THE PERSPECTIVE OF THE PATH

On the second topic, the treatise states:

> Successive, initial,
> Familiarization, perfection, [IV.17c-d]

> Concordant, conflicting,
> Separation, special,
> Superior, and unsurpassable—
> This is a summary of different fruitions. [IV.18]

These stanzas on the cultivation of remedies constitute the fourth chapter of the treatise *Distinguishing the Middle from Extremes*.

"**Successive** fruition" refers to "developing the enlightened mind based on one's potential" and the rest [of the nine states mentioned above]. The "**initial** fruition" is when supramundane qualities are obtained for the first time. The "fruition that occurs via **familiarization**" refers to all [subsequent supramundane stages of] training. The "fruition of **perfection**" is the stage beyond training. The "**concordant** fruition" refers to the causal sequence of entities. The "**conflicting** fruition" refers to the path of elimination, the initial fruition. The "fruition of **separation**" from the afflictions refers to the "fruition of familiarization" and the "fruition of perfection." The "**special** fruition" refers to the special qualities, the super-knowledges and so forth. The "**superior** fruition" refers to the grounds of the Bodhisattvas, **and** the "**unsurpassable** fruition" refers to the ground of the Buddha. **This is a summary of different fruitions.** When elaborated, they are infinite.

The cultivation of remedies can be summarized as follows: the training in purifying, the training in diminishing, the training in thoroughly purifying, the training in authentically initiating the superior, the training in merging (i.e., merging with the path of seeing), the training of entry, the supreme training, the initial training, the intermediate training, the final training, the training that involves a superior and the unsurpassable training (i.e., that which is superior with respect to its focal point, directing of the mind and attainment).

The states can be summarized as the fortunate state of having potential; the state of initiating (from developing the enlightened mind through the preparation); the states of impurity, purity, and utter purity; the ornamented state; the pervasive state (because it pervades the ten grounds); and the unsurpassable state.

The fruitions can be summarized as the condensation, its particulars, prior familiarization, evolving accomplishment, presentation, and explanation. The condensation refers to the five fruitions. The remaining fruitions are the particular instances of these five. Prior familiarization is the ripened effect. The remaining four are accomplishments related to the steady development of this ripened effect. Presentation refers to successive fruition and the rest of the four in that category. Explanation refers to concordant fruition and so forth, as these explain the [earlier four fruitions].

"Successive fruition" refers to a sequence of results, each component of which is itself a causal event, such as developing the enlightened mind based on one's potential. The "initial fruition" is the path of seeing, which is the first supramundane path to be reached. Becoming familiar with what one has seen is [also a fruition], the path of cultivation, as is the perfection of that familiarity, the final path. The first of these results is the path of inspired conduct, while the latter three results pertain to the supramundane path. The entire range of the path's results are contained within these four.

"Successive fruition" is referred to as a "concordant fruition" because its qualities accord with what preceded them and because all its stages are aspects of engaging with suchness. The path of seeing is referred to as the "conflicting fruition" because it consists of factors that conflict with the afflictions that are eliminated when [suchness] is seen. The fruitions of "familiarization" and its "perfection" are both referred to as the "fruition of separation" because they are stages of separation

from factors that obscure the grounds. The attainment of special qualities, such as the various types of super-knowledge, is referred to as the
"special fruition." The "fruition of superiority" refers to the Bodhisattva
grounds because those on these grounds are superior to the Listeners
and Self-realized Buddhas. The ground of buddhahood is referred to as
the "unsurpassable fruition."

This way of enumerating the fruitions differs from the enumeration
given above, which explained "becoming a vessel" and four other categories. The fruitions explained in these two sections summarize and provide
general categories for the fruitions of the entire range of paths. When divided extensively, however, the results of the three vehicles are limitless.

This was the commentary to the fourth chapter of the treatise
Distinguishing the Middle from Extremes, the stanzas on the cultivation of
remedies.

FIVE
THE UNSURPASSABLE VEHICLE

The second section contains a discussion of the unique path of the Great Vehicle. This section includes (1) a brief presentation, and (2) detailed explanation.

BRIEF PRESENTATION

On the first topic, the treatise states:

> **Its unsurpassability is held**
> **To lie in practice, observation,**
> **And true accomplishment. [V.1a-c]**

The Unsurpassable Vehicle should be explained next and so it is said: **Its unsurpassability is held to lie in** [this vehicle's] unsurpassable **practice,** unsurpassable **observation, and** unsurpassable **true accomplishment.**

The significance of the Unsurpassable Vehicle is held to lie in its unsurpassable practice, unsurpassable observation, and unsurpassable true accomplishment.

DETAILED EXPLANATION

The second section presents a detailed explanation, which covers (1) unsurpassable practice, (2) unsurpassable observation, and (3) unsurpassable true accomplishment. The first of these includes two further divisions: (1) a brief presentation, and (2) detailed explanation.

UNSURPASSABLE PRACTICE

BRIEF PRESENTATION

On the first topic, the treatise states:

> There are six kinds of practice [V.1d]
> That relate to the transcendences:[38]
>
> The eminent and directing the mind;
> Concordant factors and eliminating the two extremes;
> The specific and the general. [V.2a-c]

There are six kinds of **practice that relate to** practicing **the transcendences**: the **eminent** practice **and** the practice of **directing the mind**,
the practice of **concordant factors and** the practice of **eliminating extremes**, the **specific** practice **and the general** practice.

There are six types of unsurpassable practice that allow one to accomplish the six or ten transcendences. What are these six practices? They
are the practices of (1) eminence, (2) directing the mind, (3) concordant
factors, (4) eliminating dualistic extremes, (5) the specific, and (6) the
general.

THE EMINENT PRACTICE

Of the five topics listed above,[39] the first is eminent practice. This section
explains (1) the form of practice—the twelve types of eminence, and (2)
what is practiced—the ten transcendences.

THE TWELVE TYPES OF EMINENCE

On the first topic, the treatise states:

> The eminent is asserted to have [V.2d]
>
> A twelvefold nature: in its vastness,
> Endurance, pursuit, inexhaustibility,
> Continuity, ease, mastery,
> Embrace, commencement, [V.3]

Attainment, causal link,
And accomplishment. [V.4a-b]

The eminent [practice of this vehicle] **is asserted to have a twelvefold nature.** It is (1) eminent **in its vastness,** as one does not desire any type of worldly abundance, but instead practices that which perfectly transcends the world; (2) eminent in terms of **endurance,** since one must apply oneself diligently for three incalculable eons; (3) eminent in its **pursuit,** which entails working for the welfare of all sentient beings; (4) eminent in the **inexhaustibility** [of the virtue it generates], as [this virtue] is fully dedicated to great enlightenment; (5) eminent in its **continuity,** since generosity and the other transcendences are fully perfected by seeing oneself and others as equal; (6) eminent in its **ease,** as these same transcendences are fully perfected simply by rejoicing in the generosity and other [virtuous acts] of others; (7) eminent in its **mastery,** insofar as generosity and the other transcendences are fully perfected via factors such as the treasury of space, a type of meditative absorption; (8) eminent in [the way the transcendences] are **embrace**d by non-conceptual wakefulness; (9) eminent in its **commencement,** since one's acceptance of the selfless nature [of all phenomena] develops on the ground of inspired conduct; (10) eminent in its **attainment,** as the first ground is attained; (11) eminent in the way that the second to ninth grounds are **causa**lly **link**ed [with the transcendences]; **and (12)** eminent in its **accomplishment,** the achievement of the tenth ground and buddhahood.

The Bodhisattva path consists of engaging in and practicing the transcendences. It is superior to the path of the Listeners and Self-realized Buddhas in various ways, including its eminent practice. In what ways can this practice be said to be "eminent"? Its eminence can be characterized in terms of twelve qualities: (1) It is eminently vast, insofar as the Bodhisattva engages the vast qualities that transcend the world without wishing for any mundane abundance. (2) It involves eminent endurance, as one must remain diligent for three incalculable eons. (3) It is an eminent pursuit, since one practices in order to benefit an infinite number of beings. (4) It is eminent in its inexhaustibility, since [the merit it generates] is dedicated to great enlightenment, thus ensuring that it is not exhausted, even if nothing remains of the aggregates. (5) Its continuity is eminent, since the virtue is perfected in unbroken continuity due to one's conviction in the equality of self and other. (6) It is eminently easy, in the sense that one can totally perfect generosity and the other transcendences through skillful methods like rejoicing. (7) The mastery it entails is eminent, as factors like the meditative absorption of the treasury of space allow one to bring the transcendences to a state of culmination, just as one desires. (8) Generosity and the other transcendences are embraced in an eminent way by non-conceptual wakefulness. The way in which the transcendences are practiced in a vast and profound manner via these eight makes [this vehicle] especially exalted.

The remaining four principles are presented with reference to the stages in practice that involve these eight features. (9) It is eminent in its commencement, referring to the acceptance of emptiness that develops on the paths of accumulation and joining. (10) Its attainment is eminent, referring to the initial attainment of the path that transcends the world on the first ground. (11) It is eminent insofar as it accords with the cause, in that the gradual manifestation that takes place on the second to the ninth grounds is causally linked with the transcendences. (12) Its accomplishment is eminent, which is held to refer to the final Bodhisattva stage, the tenth ground, as well as the accomplishment of buddhahood, the eleventh ground of the Thus Gone One.

THE TEN TRANSCENDENCES

The second section deals with that which is practiced [in this vehicle], the ten transcendences. This includes (1) a brief presentation, and (2) detailed explanation.

BRIEF PRESENTATION

On the first topic, the treatise states:

> Thus, the ten transcendences are asserted
> With reference to their eminent character. [V.4c-d]

Thus, the ten transcendences are asserted to be classified with reference to their twelve kinds of eminent character.

The ten transcendences are held to be eminent and supreme because they are eminent in the twelve ways described above. They are called "transcendences" because they are beyond the inferior, ordinary level that is not eminent.

DETAILED EXPLANATION

The second section contains a detailed explanation that addresses (1) the essence of the transcendences, and (2) their function.

THE ESSENCE OF THE TRANSCENDENCES

On the first topic, the treatise states:

> Generosity, discipline, patience, diligence,
> Concentration, knowledge, means,
> Aspiration, power, and wakefulness—
> These are the ten transcendences. [V.5]

Some may wonder what these ten are. For this reason, their names are taught as follows: **generosity, discipline, patience, diligence, concentration, knowledge, means, aspiration, power, and wakefulness—** these are the ten transcendences.

What are the ten transcendences? (1) Generosity, giving without attachment; (2) discipline, not failing to apply oneself to accepting and rejecting in the correct manner; (3) patience, being unaffected by anger and the other factors that conflict with it and free from becoming upset; (4) diligence, taking joy in virtue and practicing it consistently; (5) concentration, the mind's resting one-pointedly and not moving from its focal point; (6) knowledge, clearly discerning [the nature of] all phenomena; (7) skillful means, which allows one to accomplish great benefit for oneself and others with ease; (8) aspiration, gathering vast accumulations of virtue without interruption; (9) power, which keeps fundamental virtues from dissipating and subdues conflicting factors; and (10) the wakefulness that penetrates the ultimate meaning in accordance with the principles of the Great Vehicle's intent.

THE FUNCTION OF THE TRANSCENDENCES

On the second topic, the treatise states:

Their functions are to care,
Avoid harm and tolerate it,
Develop good qualities, have the ability to lead,
Bring about liberation,
Remain inexhaustible, practice continuously,
Be certain, enjoy and ripen. [V.6]

Their specific functions are to do the following: The Bodhisattvas' generosity is what makes them **care** for all sentient beings. Discipline allows them to **avoid harm**ing sentient beings **and** patience enables them to **tolerate it** when others harm them. Diligence helps them to **develop good qualities**. With concentration, they **have the ability to lead** others through the gate of the Dharma by inspiring them with miraculous feats and so forth. Knowledge allows them to **bring about liberation** by granting genuine instructions. Skillful means, whereby the fundamental virtues that are accumulated are dedicated to great enlightenment, ensure that these virtues **remain inexhaustible**. Aspiration leads to rebirths that are conducive [to practice]. This, in turn, allows the Bodhisattvas to please the Buddhas and **practice** the transcendences **continuously** in all their lives. Power allows the Bodhisattva to **be certain** with respect to their practice of generosity and the other transcendences, since the power of their discerning realization and meditation keeps the conflicting factors at bay. With transcendent wakefulness, there is no confusion concerning the explicit teachings of the Dharma. This leads them to **enjoy** the Dharma, generosity, and the other transcendences **and** also to totally **ripen** sentient beings.

The functions of the ten transcendences are as follows: Generosity ensures that beings are satisfied and cared for. Discipline keeps others from being harmed, as it entails giving up harming others as well as the basis for such acts. Patience allows one to tolerate harmful situations. With diligence, good qualities develop. Displaying super-knowledges, miraculous powers, and other abilities associated with concentration gives one the capacity to make others enter the Teachings. Knowledge enables one to teach the Dharma in a way that completely liberates others. Through dedication and other forms of skillful means, the fundamental virtues that are accumulated will not be exhausted. Aspiration secures a fortunate rebirth, on the basis of which the practice of generosity and so on will be sustained. As power conquers the conflicting factors, it becomes certain that the fundamental virtues that are accumulated will lead to enlightenment. Through wakefulness, one will be able to enjoy generosity and the other aspects of the path of the Great Vehicle in a faultless manner, thereby maturing other sentient beings.

DIRECTING THE MIND

The second section explains the practice of directing the mind. This covers (1) the concise approach—directing the mind using the three types of knowledge, and (2) the extensive approach—directing the mind via the ten Dharma activities.

THE THREE TYPES OF KNOWLEDGE

The first of these topics includes presentations of (1) the three types of knowledge, and (2) their function.

THE ACTUAL TYPES OF KNOWLEDGE

On the first topic, the treatise states:

> The topics designated in the Great Vehicle—
> To these, the Bodhisattvas
> Always direct their minds
> Using three types of knowledge. [V.7]

What is the practice of directing the mind? **The topics designated in** the sūtras and other scriptures of **the Great Vehicle** concern generosity and the other transcendences. **To these, the Bodhisattvas always** practice **directing their minds using the three types of knowledge** that come from study, reflection, and meditation.

What do Bodhisattvas direct their minds towards? They direct their minds to the various topics designated in the Great Vehicle. The sūtras, hymns, and other scriptures of the Great Vehicle present a multitude of vast and profound topics. The topics that are presented, or designated, in these scriptures are the three doors of liberation, the ten transcendences, the ten grounds, the five paths, the retentions, the absorptions, and so on. Without error, a Bodhisattva directs his or her mind to these topics just as they are taught. How so? It should be understood that Bodhisattvas use three forms of knowledge to direct their minds continually to their focal point, the meaning of these vast and profound topics. These three forms of knowledge come from study, reflection, and meditation, respectively.

THE FUNCTION OF THE THREE TYPES OF KNOWLEDGE

On the second topic, the treatise states:

> **The element is strengthened, one applies oneself,**
> **And through that, the objectives are accomplished. [V.8a-b]**

What qualities are attained by directing the mind using these three knowledges? When directing the mind via the knowledge that comes from study, **the element** [of enlightenment] **is strengthened.** Through reflection **one** sincerely **applies oneself** to the meaning one has studied. **And through that,** the knowledge that comes from meditation, **the objectives are accomplished.**

Directing one's mind by studying the topics of the Great Vehicle in a precise manner strengthens and develops the qualities of one's [spiritual] potential, the element [of enlightenment]. The knowledge that comes from reflection brings about a committed engagement with these topics. Directing the mind through meditation brings about the perfect accomplishment of all the objectives that are pursued on the Bodhisattva path. Thus, once the grounds have been entered, one will gradually accomplish the final fruition.

THE TEN DHARMA ACTIVITIES

The second topic contains (1) a brief presentation, and (2) detailed explanation.

BRIEF PRESENTATION

On the first topic, the treatise states:

> **It must be understood that this is encompassed**
> **Totally by the ten Dharma activities: [V.8c-d]**

It must be understood that this accomplishment of directing the mind, which allows one to practice in a way that grants access to the grounds, **is encompassed totally by the ten Dharma activities.**

When classified extensively, directing the mind to the topics of the Great Vehicle should be known to be totally encompassed by the ten Dharma activities.

DETAILED EXPLANATION

The second section includes (1) a presentation of the essence and benefits of the ten Dharma activities, and (2) an explanation of the unique benefits associated with the Dharma activities of the Great Vehicle.

THE TEN DHARMA ACTIVITIES

On the first topic, the treatise states:

> To transcribe letters, make offerings,
> Give generously, listen, read,
> Memorize, explain, recite,
> Reflect, and meditate. [V.9]
>
> The nature of these ten activities involves
> An immeasurable accumulation of merit [V.10a-b]

What are the ten Dharma activities? To (1) **transcribe** the **letters** of the Great Vehicle's [scriptures], (2) **make offerings** to them, (3) **give generously** to others, (4) **listen** to [the scriptures of] the Great Vehicle when they are being read aloud by others, (5) **read** [such scriptures] oneself, (6) **memorize** their words, (7) **explain** their words and meaning to others, (8) **recite** their words, (9) **reflect** on their meaning, and (10) **meditate** by correctly directing one's mind [to this meaning]. **The nature of these ten Dharma activities involves an immeasurable accumulation of merit.**

The ten categories alluded to above condense all the various approaches to practicing and engaging in the sacred Dharma. What are these ten? They are (1) transcribing the words that form the basis of the sacred

Dharma, which is comprised of the Great and the Lesser Vehicles; (2-3) making offerings to and giving generously to the Dharma and those who teach it; (4) making use of one's ear faculty to listen to the words of the Dharma; (5) reading Dharma books; (6) memorizing the words that express [the Dharma]; (7) explaining their meaning to others; (8) chanting from memory; (9) taking the meaning to heart; and (10) meditating on this meaning single-pointedly and in the correct manner. It is taught that these ten Dharma activities condense every activity that relates to the sacred Dharma and that each entails an immeasurable amount of merit.

The sacred Dharma is the source of all benefit and happiness and is the path that transcends the world. Therefore, any action linked to it is extremely meaningful. The value of writing or hearing a single verse is widely praised in the sūtras as being superior to any mundane fundamental virtue.

THE DHARMA ACTIVITIES OF THE GREAT VEHICLE

On the second topic, the treatise states:

> Due to superiority and inexhaustibility;
> Due to its benefit to others and not ceasing. [V.10c-d]

Why do the sūtras teach that practicing the Dharma via the Great Vehicle accomplishes such a vast result, whereas this does not occur in the Vehicle of the Listeners? It is **due to superiority and inexhaustibility**. In other words, it should be understood that this vehicle is superior **due to its** practices, which bring **benefit to others and** because its results are inexhaustible, as the bodies and wakefulnesses are **not ceasing**, they are not disrupted, even in the total transcendence of suffering.

In the sūtras of the Thus Gone One, the Dharma activities of the Great Vehicle are singled out for praise. Why is this? It is because transcribing the teachings of the Great Vehicle and the rest of the ten Dharma activities are comparatively superior to those practiced in the Lesser Vehicle. How so? They are superior because the path of the Great Vehicle is superior to that of the Listeners. Also, the fruition of this path consists of qualities that defy the imagination; these qualities, which include the bodies and wakefulnesses, do not become exhausted in the basic field where nothing of the aggregates remains. Hence, the Dharma that teaches such a path and fruition is distinctively superior. Likewise, the benefits of writing and the other activities are also superior when they relate to such Dharma.

What was just explained is indeed the case, because the path of the Listeners [aims] merely to benefit the individual practitioner. The path of the Great Vehicle, in contrast, focuses primarily on the welfare of others. Consequently, the latter results in activity that remains unceasing and uninterrupted as long as there are sentient beings.

CONCORDANT FACTORS

The third section addresses the practice of concordant factors, which includes (1) a brief presentation, and (2) detailed explanation.

BRIEF PRESENTATION

On the first topic, the treatise states:

> Being undistracted and unmistaken—
> These are the concordant factors. [V.11a-b]

How does one practice the concordant factors? By **being undistracted and unmistaken—these are the concordant factors.**

How does one practice the Dharma in accordance with Dharma? Calm abiding keeps one from being distracted from the object one is focusing on, while insight perceives the nature of entities in an unerring way. These two are referred to as the "practice of concordant factors" for the following reason. These practices are in harmony with the precise meaning of the Great Vehicle's Dharma, which can be accurately resolved from its teachings. That is to say, stainless knowledge that is supported by undistracted meditative absorption has the capacity to realize the nature of entities in an unerring manner. Therefore, calm abiding and insight enable one to bring the meaning of the Dharma into one's own experience.

DETAILED EXPLANATION

The second section includes discussions of (1) undistracted calm abiding, and (2) unmistaken insight.

CALM ABIDING

On the first topic, the treatise states:

> Emergence and engagement in objects,
> Savoring, dullness and agitation, [V.11c-d]

> The trusting mind,
> Directing the mind while fixating on the ego,
> And the lesser mindset—these are what the wise
> Must understand to be distraction. [V.12]

Non-distraction is when the six distractions are absent. The six distractions are as follows: (1) Inherent distraction refers to the five collections of consciousness [that bring about one's] **emergence** from absorption, **and** (2) external distraction refers to **engagement in objects**. (3) Internal distraction involves **savoring** [the experience of] absorption, as well as **dullness and agitation**. (4) Distraction of marks is **the trusting mind** that apprehends marks with respect to the [absorption]. (5) Distraction that occurs through negative tendencies involves **directing the mind while fixating on the ego, and** (6) distraction in directing the mind with **the lesser mindset** is [the motivation] of the Lesser Vehicle. **These are what the wise must understand to be distraction.**

What is undistracted calm abiding? It is meditative absorption free of the six types of distraction. What are these six? (1) Inherent distraction refers to the eye consciousness and the other four collections of consciousness. Because they are naturally directed outward, they [cause one to] emerge from meditative absorption. (2) External distraction refers to a mental consciousness that reaches out towards or engages objects. (3) Internal distraction concerns dullness and agitation, as well as savoring one's meditative absorption. (4) The distraction of marks occurs when, trusting in meditative absorption, one apprehends marks of it and becomes attached. (5) Distraction brought about by negative tendencies is when directing the mind involves the apprehending of an ego. This is said to refer to the mental act of pridefully believing oneself to be superior to others, or [simply any mental act] that involves apprehending an "I." (6) The distraction of directing the mind occurs when one is caught up in the mindset of, and directs the mind in the style of, the Lesser Vehicle.

The undistracted calm abiding that is determined by the elimination of those six is the unique calm abiding of the Great Vehicle. This is a state of one-pointed inner rest, a flawless calm abiding. In it, there is no apprehension of marks, as is the case when inner absorption alone is believed to bring liberation. Neither does it involve the ego apprehension that occurs in the concentrations of non-Buddhists. Further, one does not direct the mind as one would when cultivating the supports for the inferior paths [to liberation]. This is how the wise should understand the calm abiding of the Great Vehicle.

INSIGHT

The second topic includes (1) a brief presentation, and (2) detailed explanation.

BRIEF PRESENTATION

On the first topic, the treatise states:

> Syllables, meanings, mental activity,
> Freedom from conceptual constructs, the two characteristics,
> Purity and impurity, the adventitious,
> Fearlessness, and lack of conceit. [V.13]

It should be understood that there are ten ways of being unmistaken: being unmistaken about (1) syllables, (2) meanings, (3) mental activity, (4) freedom from conceptual constructs, (5-6) the two characteristics (the general and specific), (7) purity and impurity, (8) the adventitious, (9) fearlessness, and (10) lack of conceit.

In the Great Vehicle, insight entails the correct realization of all things, both as they are and as they appear. This can be summarized under ten topics: being unmistaken regarding (1) syllables, (2) meanings, (3) mental activity, (4) freedom from conceptual constructs, (5) the specific characteristic and (6) the general characteristic, (7) purity and impurity, (8) the adventitious, (9) fearlessness, and (10) lack of conceit.

DETAILED EXPLANATION

In this second section, the ten topics covered in the brief presentation are expanded upon. These are (1) being unmistaken regarding syllables, the medium for expression; (2) being unmistaken regarding the meaning they express, which is imaginary and lacks any nature; (3) being unmistaken regarding mental activity, the mere awareness of the dependent nature, the cause of dualistic appearances; (4) being unmistaken by not constructing the two extremes, which occurs through realizing dualistic appearance to be illusory and false; (5) being unmistaken about the thoroughly established nature's specific characteristic, its absence of apprehended and apprehender; (6) being unmistaken about the general characteristic of phenomena, knowing that no phenomenon lies outside this non-dual reality; (7) being unmistaken about the purity and impurity that are based on realizing or not realizing reality; (8) being unmistaken with the knowledge that because the nature [of phenomena] is pure, the appearances of purity and impurity are adventitious; (9) being unmistaken regarding the original purity [of all phenomena], which ensures that one need not fear being obscured by the thoroughly afflictive; and (10) being unmistaken in understanding that because [the qualities of] complete purification do not develop, there is no [basis for] feeling conceited about having such special qualities.

SYLLABLES

On the first topic, the treatise states:

> **Connection and familiarity,**
> **Lack of connection and no familiarity:**
> **Due to the first two, meaning is present and to the latter two,**
> **   it is not—**
> **This is being unmistaken about syllables. [V.14]**

Syllables [convey meaning] when they are expressed with an uninter-rupted **connection** between them **and** when there is **familiarity** with the particular expression. On the other hand, when the opposite is the case and there is a **lack of** such **connection and no familiarity**, [the syl-lables do not convey any meaning]. Thus, **due to the first two, mean-ing is present and to the latter two, it is not**—[understanding] **this is being unmistaken about syllables.**

There are two factors that lend meaning to the syllables that express [this meaning]. First, syllables must be correctly connected with one another in a sequence. Second, once linguistic symbols have been set forth based on these syllables, the mind must be familiar with the way a given linguistic symbol is associated with a particular meaning. Take the word "pillar," for example. When the two syllables in this word are arranged and pronounced in the customary order, "pil-lar," one will understand [that this refers to] an entity that performs the function of supporting beams. If the sequence were reversed so that "lar" were stated before "pil," or if the syllables were expressed separately without being linked with one another, they would be unable to convey this meaning. Hence, these two syllables are set forth in this way as a linguistic symbol for something that functions to support beams. English speakers[40] who have previously familiarized themselves with this particular term will be able to derive meaning from its use. However, this would not necessarily be the case with those from foreign lands. Therefore, it is these two factors that make a linguistic symbol meaningful: connection and familiarity. Alternatively, when there is no connection or familiarity, syllables will not convey any meaning.

Understanding correctly in this way is being unmistaken regarding syllables. When a meaning is understood through a linguistic symbol composed of syllables, it is because people have made designations based on connections they themselves created; they were not there to begin with. There is no intrinsic relationship between a name and its meaning. This [type of insight] allows one unerringly to ascertain the way in which meanings are understood from syllables. Based on this, Bodhisattvas come to understand that ultimately words do not express any meaning.

MEANING

On the second topic, the treatise states:

> Dualistic appearances
> Are not what they seem.
> This is being unmistaken about the meaning
> That transcends existence and non-existence. [V.15]

The **dualistic appearances** of apprehended and apprehender **are not what they seem;** [they do not exist] in the way they appear. Seeing the meaning in **this** way **is being unmistaken about the meaning that transcends** both the **existence** of apprehended and apprehending entities **and** the **non-existence** of the delusive appearance of such entities.

The dualistic appearances of apprehended and apprehender do not exist as they appear. They appear, yet are unreal. Realizing this is referred to as "being unmistaken about the meaning." This meaning, or nature, transcends the extreme of existence because duality is unestablished. It transcends the extreme of non-existence because the mere appearance [of duality] does exist. Based on this, a realization free of apprehended and apprehender arises.

MENTAL ACTIVITY

On the third topic, the treatise states:

> Infusion with concepts forms the basis
> For conceptual mental activity.
> This is being unmistaken about mental activity
> That causes the appearance of duality. [V.16]

Thorough **infusion with** the **concepts** of apprehended and apprehender **forms the basis for conceptual mental activity.** [Understanding] **this is being unmistaken about mental activity.** What type of mental activity is one unmistaken about? It is with respect to mental activity **that causes the appearance of duality** or, in other words, conceptual mental activity suffused with mistaken notions formed [in the past].

Because [the mind] is suffused with concepts of apprehended and apprehender formed in the past, subsequent concepts arise and appear as places, objects, and bodies. This forms the basis for mental activity. When this is understood correctly, one is said to be "unmistaken regarding mental activity"; to have realized the nature of mental activity, of mere conceptuality, just as it is.

What is the basis, or foundation, of this mental activity? It is understood to be caused by the all-ground consciousness, the cause of dualistic appearance. Considering the fact that it is the causal [foundation] for the infusion of all manner of concepts, it is termed the "all-ground of various habitual tendencies." This consciousness is termed the "all-ground of maturation," considering how the myriad of internal and external phenomena manifest through its power. Hence, the all-ground is the cause of everything.

FREEDOM FROM CONCEPTUAL CONSTRUCTS

On the fourth topic, the treatise states:

> In actuality non-existent, yet existent,
> They are held to be like illusions and so forth.
> This is being unmistaken regarding freedom from conceptual
>   constructs
> Since there is no conceptual construction of existence or non-
>   existence. [V.17]

The things explained above are **in actuality non-existent, yet existent**. Therefore, **they are held to be like illusions**, dreams, mirages, reflections of the moon in water, and **so forth**. While none of these exist as entities, the mere delusion [of such an existence] is not non-existent either. As it sees that they in fact resemble illusions and so forth, the mind does not create conceptual constructs. This type of seeing **is being unmistaken regarding freedom from conceptual constructs, since there is no conceptual construction of existence or non-existence**.

All phenomena subsumed under apprehended and apprehender are intrinsically non-existent; this is their actual nature. Nevertheless, they do exist as mere appearances. In this way, they are held to be like illusions, dreams, and so on. This is what is meant by being unmistaken regarding freedom from conceptual constructs because as one avoids falling into one-sided positions in this way, [believing phenomena to be] either existent or non-existent, conceptual constructions do not occur.

THE SPECIFIC CHARACTERISTIC

On the fifth topic, the treatise states:

> Because no concepts apply,
> Everything is purely nominal.

This is being unmistaken about the specific characteristic,
The ultimate specific characteristic. [V.18]

Because no concepts apply, everything that is spoken of as "eye" and
"form," up to "mind" and "[mental] phenomena," is purely nominal.
This understanding is being unmistaken about the specific characteristic. About what type of characteristic? One is unmistaken about the
ultimate specific characteristic, since at [the level of] the relative one
does not think, "everything is purely nominal!"

None of the concepts of apprehended and apprehender apply to the
specific characteristic of [phenomena's] real nature. This is because the
ultimate object of individual self-aware wakefulness is the pacification
of all constructs. This kind of nature does not contain various divisions.
All the appearances of different types of phenomena, whatever they may
be, are not established as distinct, specific characteristics, despite their
appearance. In reality, they are without any essence of their own; they are
nothing more than nominal designations. Thus, the specific characteristic
of all phenomena is emptiness.

Understanding this is what is called "being unmistaken regarding specific characteristics." At the level of worldly convention, the appearances
of distinct features may be referred to by speaking of the specific characteristics of pillars, vases, and so on. Here, however, the [term] "specific
characteristic" is used to refer to the specific characteristic of the ultimate—the way all phenomena are.

THE GENERAL CHARACTERISTIC

On the sixth topic, the treatise states:

Apart from the basic field of phenomena
There are no phenomena.
Therefore, this is being unmistaken
About the general characteristic. [V.19]

Apart from the basic field of phenomena, the nature of which is
the selflessness of phenomena, there are no phenomena whatsoever.
Therefore, this understanding is being unmistaken about the general
characteristic.

By nature, the basic field of phenomena is empty of duality. There are no "phenomena" whatsoever apart from this basic field because this basic field is the nature of all phenomena. For this reason, the basic field of phenomena is the general characteristic that pervades all phenomena. Knowing this is to be unmistaken regarding the general characteristic.

IMPURITY AND PURITY

On the seventh topic, the treatise states:

> Based on whether or not mistaken mental activity
> Has been eliminated,
> It is either impure or pure.
> This is being unmistaken about that. [V.20]

Based on whether or not mistaken mental activity has been eliminated, it (the basic field of phenomena) **is either impure or pure. This** understanding **is being unmistaken about that** (impurity and purity).

Though we may speak of cyclic existence and the transcendence of suffering, purity and impurity, they are not established in an objectively distinct way, not in the slightest. Rather, purity and impurity are spoken of with reference to someone who has eliminated the view of self and other forms of mistaken mental activity, and someone who has not. Understanding this is being unmistaken regarding the meaning of purity and impurity.

THE ADVENTITIOUS

On the eighth topic, the treatise states:

> The basic field of phenomena is pure by nature
> And, therefore, like space.
> The two are adventitious occurrences.
> This is being unmistaken with respect to that. [V.21]

The basic field of phenomena is pure by nature and, therefore, like space. The two, impurity and subsequent purity, **are adventitious oc-**

currences. Understanding this is being unmistaken with respect to
that, the latter being the adventitious occurrence of these two.

Because the basic field of phenomena is completely pure by nature,
like space, it never changes. This is the way things are, their innate nature.
Occurrences of impurity and subsequent purity happen adventitiously;
merely in terms of how things appear. To understand this is to be unmistaken about the adventitious.

FEARLESSNESS AND ABSENCE OF CONCEIT

On the ninth and tenth topics, the treatise states:

> Because they do not exist, persons and phenomena
> Are neither afflicted nor purified.
> Thus, there is no fear and no ego.
> This is being unmistaken with respect to that. [V.22]

Because they do not exist, persons and phenomena are neither afflicted nor purified. Thus, there is no fear and no ego-centered pride.
This is being unmistaken with respect to that fearlessness and absence
of conceit.

Because they are devoid of any essence, the nature of both phenomena
and beings is free from thorough affliction and complete purification. As
exemplified by space, that which has no essence can neither be bound by
afflictions nor liberated from them. In terms of the way things truly are,
there is not a single phenomenon that is afflicted or purified. Therefore,
there is [no basis] to the fear that attachment and other factors of thorough affliction will develop, nor [are there any grounds] for feeling conceited about the development of faith and the other factors of complete
purification. The reason for this is that there are no observable bases for
fear or pride. This is what is meant by being unmistaken about fearlessness and the absence of pride.

THE TEN VAJRA STATEMENTS

Next follows a supplementary commentary, consisting of (1) a summary,
or concise presentation, of the content related to these ten ways of be-

ing unmistaken, and (2) a presentation of these ten via ten vajra statements.[41]

Summary

On the first topic, the treatise states:

What delusion concerns, is, and is based on;
What the absence of delusion is and concerns.
The results of delusion and its absence,
And the end of these two.

These can be understood in detail by means of ten vajra statements. The content of these vajra statements is classified into five divisions: (1) three essential natures, (2) observation, (3) non-conceptuality, (4) objection, and (5) reply. **What delusion concerns** is the thoroughly established nature. The imaginary nature is what delusion **is. And** the dependent nature is what delusion **is based on.** Knowledge is **what the** non-conceptual **absence of delusion is and** natural luminosity is what it **concerns.** [Moreover, there are] **the results of delusion and its absence, and the end of these two.**

The meaning that is summarized by the vajra statements is as follows: The three essential natures are the observation. The first three statements correspond with these three. Respectively, these three are "the thoroughly established," "the imaginary," and "the dependent."

[When we speak of] non-conceptuality, why is non-conceptuality non-conceptual? Because of [the presence of] non-conceptual wakefulness. And what is it that is not conceptualized? It is the very [nature of] natural luminosity that isn't conceptualized. Hence, the classifications of cognition and object of cognition should be understood to correspond to the three essential natures and non-conceptuality.

The remaining vajra statements present objections and replies. The first objection is as follows: If no properties of imaginary or dependent characteristics exist, then how can they be observed? If they do exist, then it does not make sense for phenomena to be natural luminosity. In response, it is said that they are just like an illusion; like an illusory creation, they do not exist, yet can still be observed.

One may then object: If phenomena are natural luminosity, then how can there first be thorough affliction and then complete purification later on? In reply, it is said that thorough affliction and complete purification must be understood to be like space. [Associating the intrinsic nature with such terms is,] in other words, like declaring space to be "thoroughly afflicted" and "completely purified," despite its pure nature.

Then, it may be argued: If countless Buddhas appear and dispel the thorough afflictions of countless sentient beings, then why isn't the continuity of cyclic existence interrupted and why doesn't the transcendence of suffering expand? The reply is that there is no decline [with regard to cyclic existence] and no superiority [with regard to the attainment of complete purification], for the realms of sentient beings and the factors of complete purification are immeasurable.

The content of these ten ways of being unmistaken, the ten vajra statements, can be presented in two ways. The first consists of four categories: observation, non-conceptuality, objection, and reply. That which is observed or cognized is explained by the first three [of the ten ways of being unmistaken], with reference to the three essential natures. Non-conceptuality is taught primarily in terms of the observing mind. It encompasses two points, [the fifth and the sixth ways of being unmistaken]. [The fifth way of] being unmistaken, which concerns specific characteristics, is explained from the perspective of a subject that does not conceptualize. [The sixth,] on the other hand, being unmistaken about the general characteristic, is explained with reference to natural luminosity, that which [the subject] does not form concepts about.

The remaining five points all relate to objections and replies [to the previous statements]. The vajra statement that explains thorough affliction and complete purification, the way of being unmistaken regarding purity and impurity, can [be understood with respect to the following exchange. First the objections]: If thorough affliction did not exist, how could it be observed? If it does exist, then there cannot be natural purity! Furthermore, if numerous Buddhas have dispelled the afflictions of an infinite number of beings, why hasn't the continuity of cyclic existence been interrupted? And why hasn't the transcendence of suffering evolved? All such doubts stem from the point regarding purity and impurity. Therefore, this [seventh] point is, as it were, the topic of dispute.

To these come four replies: The [first of these is] the reply of illusion, [the fourth vajra statement.][42] This explains that although neither object nor subject actually exists, they still appear. It may then be objected that if purity is natural, then there couldn't be any previous involvement with affliction. This is answered with [the eighth vajra statement,] the reply of space. This reply explains that although space is naturally pure, it still makes sense for it to appear to be otherwise due to the presence or absence of adventitious factors, the clouds.

[The ninth and the tenth vajra statements concern] the absence of obscurations and absence of superiority, respectively. They are associated with the reply to the following objection: Let us assume that there is impurity to begin with and that this impurity is then later purified. Since this purity is [supposed to be] irreversible and not subject to any future obscuration, why isn't the continuity of cyclic existence interrupted and why wouldn't transcendence evolve? In response, it is said that due to the fact that they have no established nature, affliction and purification have no limits. Thus, it is explained that the [way things truly are] can be neither obscured nor measured.

It is said that observation, the first of the five categories introduced above, is taught in terms of the three natures, so that the first three vajra statements refer to the thoroughly established, the imaginary, and the dependent, respectively. The way that the first, existence and non-existence, is linked to the thoroughly established nature is as follows: Syllables become meaningful when they are connected with each other and one is familiar with these constructions. No expression, therefore, takes place in terms of the essential nature. Understanding this enables one to encounter the ineffable nature of the thoroughly established nature.

In this context, certain Indians explain that the teachings of the Great Vehicle, in being causally linked with the basic field of phenomena, are the remedy for being mistaken. The reason for this is that the approach of the Great Vehicle enables one to comprehend the sheer profundity of the thoroughly established nature in a flawless manner. Others explain that the words "existence and non-existence" [in the first vajra statement] refer to being unmistaken about the existence and non-existence of the thoroughly established. In other words, they maintain that this refers to how the thoroughly established nature exists as the essence of emptiness, while at the same time being a nature within which duality does not exist. In any case, both the first two points are [also] applicable to being unmistaken about the imaginary nature. Since one comprehends the nature of the thoroughly established by understanding the emptiness of the imaginary, the first two vajra statements can be seen as constituting the same key point.

The second point relates to being unmistaken, free from error, about meanings. It explains that dualistic appearances are not established the same way they appear. They are, therefore, merely imaginary. Being unmistaken regarding the basis, or mental activity, refers to the dependent nature. This nature is the basis in the sense that it is the foundation or cause of appearances. The term "dependent nature" is, however, [generally] used in consideration of the manifest, resultant aspect of appearance.

There is also another way of presenting the content of these ten points. [The supplement to the root text] reads:

> What delusion concerns, is, and is based on;
> What the absence of delusion is and concerns.
> The results of delusion and its absence,
> And the end of these two.

What does delusion concern? It concerns the inexpressible nature, which is taken to be a field that displays marks and contains relationships between words and meanings. Essentially, delusion is the mistaken experience of duality where there is none. Infused with concepts, the all-ground consciousness is the cause and basis of delusion.

In essence, the absence of delusion is twofold. First, it entails the certainty that occurs during the ensuing attainment, in which one understands that, while nothing truly exists, illusory appearances still occur. It also involves the non-conceptual wakefulness of meditative equipoise. These two are the essence of absence of delusion, in the sense of being the subject that is freed from delusion. What this freedom from delusion concerns is natural luminosity, which entails being unmistaken regarding the general characteristic, the character of the thoroughly established nature.

The result of delusion is thorough affliction. The result of non-delusion, that with which it is causally linked, is complete purification. These are taught with [the vajra statements of] "thorough affliction and complete purification" and "the resemblance to space." The former is taught from the perspective of the conventional, and the latter in terms of the ultimate.

"The end of these two" refers to the culmination of the results just explained, their two ends. Some scholars of the Noble Land hold that both affliction and purification end in the transcendence of suffering. They explain that since the transcendence of suffering is beyond development and decline, there is, in fact, no end to be reached. This, they say, is itself their culmination. Others claim that because cyclic existence is immeasurable, the end of thorough affliction entails the absence of decline and, because the transcendence of suffering is immeasurable, the end of complete purification involves the absence of superiority. What the intelligent should understand, here, is that in a general sense and from a conventional point of view, ["the end" refers to] the full extent of both cyclic existence and the transcendence of suffering. In terms of the ultimate, however, it refers to a culmination that does not involve having to eliminate or cultivate anything that is truly established.

The points contained in these ten vajra statements can be explained in a multitude of ways. Here I have clarified and explained them according to the master Sthiramati's classic treatise. These ten points unerringly explain the conventional and ultimate natures of all phenomena, those contained within cyclic existence and the transcendence of suffering. What they teach, therefore, is insight into all that there is, just as it is.

PRESENTATION OF THE TEN VAJRA STATEMENTS

On the second topic, [the supplement to the root text] states:

> Existence and non-existence,
> Being unmistaken, basis,
> Resemblance to illusion, non-conceptuality,
> Luminosity that is permanent by nature,
>
> Thorough affliction and complete purification,
> Likewise, the resemblance to space,
> The absence of obscuration, and the absence of superiority—
> These are the ten vajra statements.

1) Existence and non-existence, in terms of being unmistaken with respect to syllables; (2) being unmistaken, in terms of being unmistaken with respect to meaning; (3) basis, in terms of being unmistaken with respect to mental activity; (4) resemblance to illusion, in terms of being unmistaken with respect to not constructing the two extremes; (5) non-conceptuality, in terms of being unmistaken with respect to specific characteristics; (6) luminosity that is permanent by nature, in terms of being unmistaken with respect to general characteristics;

(7) **thorough affliction and complete purification,** in terms of being unmistaken with respect to impurity and purity; likewise, **(8) the resemblance to space,** in terms of being unmistaken with respect to adventitious occurrences; (9) **the absence of obscuration,** in terms of being unmistaken with respect to fearlessness; **and (10) the absence of superiority,** in terms of being unmistaken with respect to the absence conceit—**these are the ten vajra statements.**

The ten ways of being unmistaken are known as the "ten vajra statements." What, then, are these ten statements? In order, they are (1) existence and non-existence, (2) being unmistaken, (3) basis, (4) resemblance to illusion, (5) non-conceptuality, (6) naturally permanent luminosity, (7) thorough affliction and complete purification, (8) resemblance to space, (9) absence of decline, and (10) absence of superiority. These are called the "ten vajra statements" because they are hard to comprehended through a [merely] intellectual approach.

ELIMINATING DUALISTIC EXTREMES

The fourth topic, practicing to eliminate dualistic extremes, contains two groups of seven.

THE FIRST SET OF SEVEN

Presenting the first group, the treatise states:

> The extremes of being different or the same;
> Both extremists and Listeners;
> Two pairs of extremes: exaggerating and depreciating
> The status of persons and phenomena; [V.23]
>
> Extremes that relate to conflicting factors and remedies;
> Ideas of permanence and annihilation;
> The two and three that relate to apprehended and apprehender
> And thorough affliction and complete purification. [V.24]

What is the practice of eliminating extremes? [This practice involves eliminating the following views:] (1) **the extreme** views **of** the self and the aggregates **being different** from one another **or the same;** (2) **both** the extreme notion of permanence imputed by **extremists and** the extreme notion of impermanence imputed by the **Listeners**; (3-4) **two pairs of extremes: exaggerating and depreciating the status of persons and phenomena; (5) extremes that relate to conflicting factors and** their **remedies**, i.e., the idea that "things like non-virtue are thoroughly afflictive" and "things like virtue are completely purifying"; **(6)** extreme **ideas of permanence**, believing that persons or phenomena exist, **and annihilation**, believing that they don't; and (7) **the two and three that** are **related to**, respectively, the extremes of **apprehended and apprehender and** the extremes of **thorough affliction and complete purification.** The latter includes three forms of thorough affliction: afflictive, karmic, and birth-related, as well as the three types of purification that remedy them.

Abiding in the Middle Way, free from dualistic extremes, is the path of the Great Vehicle. What are these extremes? (1) Believing form and the other aggregates to be different from the self is one extreme, as is the belief that they are essentially the same. The path of the Middle Way eliminates these views by explaining that the self, up to and including the human being, does not exist. The self has no essence of its own; it is only an imputation based on the aggregates. Therefore, the "person" and all its other synonyms do not actually refer to anything. Thus, the self is not the same as the aggregates, nor is it different.

(2) The second pair of extremes concerns the belief that form and so on are permanent, as is held by extremist schools, and also the extreme belief that form and so forth are impermanent, which is held by the Listeners. The path of the Middle Way completely eliminates both of these. It involves cultivating the realization that form and so forth transcend conceptual constructions of permanence, impermanence, etc. As a sūtra states: "Form is not permanent, nor is it impermanent."

(3-4) Exaggerated notions that persons and phenomena exist essentially and depreciations that deny them at the level of convention and mere appearance. These constitute two pairs of extremes: two extremes that exaggerate the existence of persons and phenomena, such as mind, and two that depreciate the status of persons and phenomena, believing them to be non-existent. The path of the Middle Way eliminates exaggerated and depreciatory views about persons. This is taught with statements such as, "The middle between self and selflessness is not conceptual." It also eliminates exaggerated and depreciatory views of phenomena like the mind, with statements such as, "Here, there is no mind, no volition, no mentality, and no consciousness."

(5) The next set concerns the extreme views that the essential nature of conflicting factors is one of non-virtue and thorough affliction, while the essential nature of the remedies is one of virtue and complete purification. These, too, are eliminated by the path of the Middle Way, as taught with statements such as, "Here, no extreme is accepted, expressed or upheld."

(6) The extreme of permanence is the idea that selves and phenomena exist and abide self-sufficiently. The extreme of annihilation, in contrast, is the idea that they do not exist, or that their continuum is brought to an end without any connection [to a future life]. The path of the Middle Way eliminates these two, teaching statements such as, "The middle is taught to be the absence of permanence and annihilation."

(7) Furthermore, the two extremes of apprehended and apprehender and the two extremes of thorough affliction and complete purification are presented in combination, as [only] two extremes. How so? There are two extremes, one in which thorough affliction, from the link of ignorance up to that of old age and death, are conceived in terms of apprehended and apprehender and one in which complete purification, the cessation of ignorance and the rest of the twelve links, are conceived in terms of apprehended and apprehender. The path of the Middle Way eliminates these two as well, as taught with statements such as, "Ignorance and the absence of ignorance are non-dual."

There are three types of thorough affliction: the thorough affliction of affliction, the thorough affliction of karma, and the thorough affliction of birth. The first, the thorough affliction of affliction, includes view, the causal three poisons, and the pursuit of rebirth. The antidotes to these three are, respectively, understanding emptiness, the absence of marks, and the absence of aspiration. The second, thorough affliction of karma, refers to the actual formation of virtuous and non-virtuous karma. Its remedy is the understanding of non-formation. The third, thorough affliction of birth, refers to taking rebirth. This involves all the instances of mind and mental states that arise between birth and death, as well as to the continuity of rebirth—the three existences of death, birth, and the intermediate state. Their remedies are, respectively, understanding that there is no birth, no arising, and no essence.

The absence of these three types of thorough affliction is complete purification. Here, there is no attachment to purification as having an essential identity. In short, whenever there are notions of the basic field of phenomena becoming afflicted or purified, or of eliminating certain factors using remedies such as emptiness, then such apprehension of dualistic extremes can be remedied through statements like this: "Phenomena are not made empty by emptiness, they are empty by their own nature."

As long as there are extremes, in terms of something to be eliminated and its remedy, the empty and the not empty, and so forth, one will remain confined to the realm of the imaginary, the conventional, and the relative. As the essential nature of the ultimate itself, from the very outset, emptiness is totally beyond being established in any such extreme manner—it is inexpressible. Nothing is made empty by it; it is the primordial condition beyond all extremes.

THE SECOND SET OF SEVEN

The second set of seven consists of (1) a brief presentation, and (2) detailed explanation.

BRIEF PRESENTATION

On the first of these, the treatise states:

> There are held to be seven forms
> Of extreme dualistic thought: [V.25a-b]

Moreover, with respect to the existence and non-existence of entities, **there are held to be seven forms of extreme dualistic thought.**

In addition to what was explained before, it is also held that there are seven types of extreme dualistic thought, or thoughts of dualistic extremes.

DETAILED EXPLANATION

On the second section, the treatise states:

> An entity that exists or does not exist,
> Pacified and that which pacifies, [V.25c-d]

The feared and the fear of that,
Apprehended and apprehender, the genuine and the false,
Performance and inability, and lack of arising and simultaneity–
These are forms of extreme dualistic thought. [V.26]

What are these seven? (1) The view that the self is **an entity that exists or** that it **does not exist**; (2) the view that there are discards to be
pacified and remedies, **that which pacifies** them; (3) thoughts of **the
feared and** the ensuing thoughts that take **the** form of **fear of that**; (4)
thoughts of **apprehended and apprehender**; (5) thoughts of **the genuine**, the undefiling, **and the false**, the defiling; (6) thoughts about the
performance of an action that eliminates discards **and** thoughts about
its **inability** to do so; **and** (7) views that regard a **lack of arising** of the
remedy **and a simultaneity** of the discard and the arisen remedy. **These
are forms of extreme dualistic thought.**

What are the seven pairs of conceptual extremes? (1) The first two are
the extreme thoughts of entity and of non-entity. As in the following
example, these two are extensively remedied by the teachings of the path
of the Middle Way: "Emptiness is not due to a destruction of the person.
Rather, emptiness is due to emptiness. There was emptiness throughout
the past and there will be so throughout the future."
(2) There are also extreme ideas concerning the discards that are pacified and the remedies that pacify them. Such ideas are remedied by the
path of the Middle Way. This path teaches that since the discards have
no established nature, their remedies are not ultimately established either. This is taught in the following quotation: "Kāśyapa, it is like this:
Imagine that someone, fearing and dreading space, would cry, 'Do away
with space!' Kāśyapa, what do you think, would it be possible to do away
with space?"
(3) The next set of extremes concerns the idea that the three realms
of cyclic existence, the source of suffering, are to be feared, as well as
thoughts that manifest as fear and terror towards the source of suffering.
The path of the Middle Way eliminates such extremes, as taught in this
passage: "Kāśyapa, it is like this. Imagine a painter who paints a horrify-
ing demon and then falls over on his face, having fainted in fear." By
understanding the example given here, one will eliminate extremes that
concern cyclic existence, which is created by one's own thoughts, and the
fear of it.

The previous example of the sky is intended for certain groups, beginning with the Listeners. The Listeners do not fully comprehend that phenomena are empty by nature. They think phenomena are to be discarded and that emptiness is what accomplishes that. In order to dispel the fear of those who take emptiness to be the destroyer of phenomena, it is taught that just as no one can do away with space, emptiness primordially permeates all phenomena; it is their intrinsic nature. The latter example of the painter was taught so that Bodhisattvas will not grow weary of remaining for long in cyclic existence. Sthiramati's commentary contains other ways of explaining these two.

(4) There are also extreme thoughts about apprehended objects, such as form, and apprehending [faculties], such as the eye. The path of the Middle Way eliminates these two as well, as taught, for example, like this: "Kāśyapa, it is like this. It is as if, for example, the illusion created by a magician were to eat the magician himself." Although the apprehended and the apprehender appear to be separate, they are not different from one another, because both are established as mere awareness. If one of them is not established, then neither is the other. Thus, this example shows how the apprehended and the apprehender lack any actual establishment.

(5) The next set of extremes includes the ideas that the undefiling is genuine and the defiling false. The path of the Middle Way eliminates these two, as taught here: "Kāśyapa, it is like this. It is as when two sticks are rubbed together and fanned by the wind so that fire arises. As soon as there is fire, the two sticks are burned." Fire arises from two sticks that are not of the nature of fire. The fire then burns the sticks themselves. Likewise, the fire of the genuine, undefiling knowledge of the noble ones is born from the wood of discriminating concepts that are present at the time of the inauthentic, defiling paths of accumulation and joining. That fire then consumes the discriminating concepts themselves. Their disintegration is dependent origination and is, thus, like an illusion. There is nothing that can be set apart as "genuine" or "false," for none of this is established by any essence of its own.

(6) The sixth category encompasses the belief that the elimination of discards by means of their remedy, wakefulness, is essentially real as a performed action, or, alternately, that the elimination of discards takes place because wakefulness intends it to happen. These are exaggerated concepts. This also includes depreciative concepts, the thought that a remedy is unable to perform the act of eliminating a discard, or that it is inefficient. The path of the Middle Way dispels these two extremes, as explained in

the following passage: "Kāśyapa, it is like this. When an oil-lamp is lit, pitch-black darkness will disappear. The lamp certainly did not think, 'I shall clear away the pitch black darkness,' Kāśyapa, yet due to the lamp, the darkness disappears." This explains that while a lamp does not think, it still has the power to dispel darkness. Wakefulness clears away the obscurations in a similar way.

(7) The final set of extreme thoughts includes the belief that, since they have been in the mind streams of sentient beings since beginningless time, the obscurations are so hard to eliminate and so powerful that there is no opportunity for wakefulness to arise. It also includes the idea that even were a remedy to arise, it would not bring about the immediate elimination of the discard and that, therefore, remedy and discard can be simultaneous and accompany each other for an extended duration. The Middle Way dispels these two extremes as well, as demonstrated here: "Kāśyapa, it is like this. Imagine that someone lights a lamp in a home, a house, or a cottage, that has remained in darkness for 100,000 years. Kāśyapa, what do you think, will the darkness say, 'I have been here for 100,000 years and I shall therefore not leave'?" When light manifests, darkness will definitely cease. The two cannot be simultaneous. No matter how long the darkness has remained, it can still be dispelled with a lamp. Through this example, such extreme concepts are dispelled.

To conclude, all of the seven sets of paired concepts that were just explained are referred to as "forms of extreme dualistic thought" because they consist of thoughts that go against the way things are, thoughts that fall into either exaggeration or depreciation. It should be understood that the Bodhisattva's path of practicing the elimination of dualistic extremes is accomplished by gaining perfect access to the meaning of the Middle Way, which is free of all such extremes.

THE SPECIFIC AND THE GENERAL

On the fifth and sixth topics, the treatise states:

> The specific and general can be understood
> In relation to the ten grounds. [V.27a-b]

What are the specific and general practices? **The specific and general can be understood in relation to the ten grounds.** The specific refers to the specific transcendences that predominate on the individual grounds, whereas the general refers to the genuine practice of all [the transcendences that takes place] on each [of the grounds].

The specific and general practices can be understood in relation to the ten grounds. How so? Practice on the first ground focuses on generosity, the second focuses on discipline, and so on. These are referred to as the "specific practices" of each ground. Genuine practice of all the transcendences also takes place upon each of the grounds. This is called "general practice."

This completes the discussion of the unsurpassable practice of the path, which was explained via the six types of practice.

UNSURPASSABLE OBSERVATION

On the second topic, the treatise states:

> **Principles, basic field,**
> **What is practiced and practice, [V.27c-d]**

> **Comprehension, certain comprehension,**
> **Total comprehension, full realization,**
> **Total expansion, understanding, natural rest,**
> **And perfection—these are held to be what is observed. [V.28]**

The unsurpassable observations are those of (1) the designations of the Dharma, the **principles** of the twelve aspects of enlightened speech; (2) suchness, the **basic field** of phenomena; (3) **what is practiced**, the six transcendences, **and** (4) the way the path is **practiced**; (5) the **comprehension** generated by the understanding that comes from study; (6) the **certain comprehension** generated by the understanding that comes from reflection; (7) the **total comprehension** generated by the understanding that comes from meditation; (8) the **full realization** entailed in achieving the path of seeing; (9) the **total expansion** that takes place up to the seventh ground; (10) **understanding;**[43] (11) the **natural rest** of the eighth ground; **and** (12) the **perfection** of the ninth ground and beyond—**these are held to be what is observed.**

There are certain factors that, when observed, form the basis for practicing [the Great Vehicle]. What are these factors? And how is it that they are accessed through observation? The following observations are unsurpassable because they are not limited, as are those of the Listeners, for example. Rather, these reference points [are accessed] through an approach that recognizes the entire meaning of the profound and the vast.

In terms of essence, there are four observations, while in terms of stages, there are eight, thus making twelve in all. They are as follows: (1) the unerring observation of the full diversity of principles that pertain to the Dharma—the ten transcendences, the grounds, the paths, the retentions, the absorptions, and so on, and (2) the observation of their profound nature as it truly is—the natural condition of suchness, the basic field that is empty of the two types of self. These two observations take place by ascertaining the meanings of, respectively, the vast and profound, which subsume the two truths.

Next follows the observations of (3) what is to be practiced and (4) the practice itself. These two relate to the previous two categories. How so? Every aspect of the vast path is contained within the ten transcendences. Thus, the experiential application of these ten constitutes the "observation of what is practiced," the transcendences. Furthermore, when the profound basic field of phenomena is realized, the transcendences are embraced by the knowledge of realization beyond the three spheres.[44] In this way, they manifest as the superior practice of skillful means. This perspective is what is known as the "observation of the practice." It is referred to as such because the transcendences, once embraced by the knowledge that realizes the absence of the three spheres, comprise the undefiling path; they are transcendences beyond the world. The observations [of the Great Vehicle] are unsurpassable in these four ways.

This fourfold observation is gradually enhanced through the stages of the path. Thus, (5) the observation of comprehension is the observation of basic field, as well as generosity and the other transcendences, via the knowledge that comes from study. (6) The observation of certain comprehension is to observe and comprehend their meaning via the knowledge that comes from reflection, which utilizes the four types of reasoning. (7) The observation of true and total comprehension is the observation that takes place via the individual self-awareness that comes from meditation. (8) The direct perception of the basic field of phenomena on the first ground is the observation of the full realization. (9) The development of realization that happens on the second to the seventh ground is the observation of total expansion. (10) On the seventh ground, all topics of the sūtras and so forth are comprehended and there is an observation that entails the understanding of the absence of marks regarding the phenomena of existence and peace. (11) The observation of natural rest occurs on the eighth ground; it involves the absence of all effort and formations. (12) The observations of the three perfections take place on the ninth ground, tenth ground, and on the eleventh ground of buddhahood. These three are perfect wakefulness, perfect activity, and perfect purity. The observation of perfect wakefulness is brought about by the attainment of the perfect wakefulness associated with the four correct discriminations of the ninth ground.[45] The observation of perfect activity is brought about by attaining the perfect mastery of activity on the tenth ground. It is asserted that the observation of perfect purity is brought about by attaining the perfect purification of absolutely all afflictive and cognitive obscurations on the eleventh ground of buddhahood. The latter involves pure wakefulness observing, or viewing, the entire range of phenomena. This is the perception of all that there is, as it is.

UNSURPASSABLE TRUE ACCOMPLISHMENT

On the third topic, the treatise states:

> Not lacking, not abandoned,
> Not distracted, completely perfected,
> Truly engendered, developed,
> Flexibility, no abiding, no obscuration,
> And its unbroken continuity—
> These are true accomplishment. [V.29]

True accomplishment is as follows: When the conditions for the path are **not lacking**, (1) the potential is truly accomplished. When the Great Vehicle is **not abandoned**, (2) devotion is truly accomplished. When one is **not distracted** by [the mindset of] the Lesser Vehicle, (3) the engendering of the enlightened mind is truly accomplished. When the transcendences are **completely perfected**, (4) practice is truly accomplished. When the noble path has been **truly engendered**, (5) engagement with the flawless is truly accomplished. When fundamental virtues have **developed**, (6) the ripening of sentient beings is truly accomplished. When there is **flexibility** of mind, (7) the fields are truly accomplished. When there is **no abiding** in existence or peace, (8) the obtainment of prophecy is truly accomplished. When there is **no** obscuration, (9) buddhahood is truly accomplished, **and** through **its unbroken continuity,** (10) the continuous revelation of enlightenment is truly accomplished. **These are true accomplishments.**

There are ten principles concerning the temporary and ultimate accomplishments of one who has embarked on the path of the Great Vehicle, accomplishments that are distinctively superior to the attainments of the Listeners and Self-realized Buddhas. These ten summarize the entire meaning of the Great Vehicle. As taught in the *Ornament of the Sūtras*:

> Potential, devotion to the Dharma,
> Development of the enlightened mind,
> Practice of generosity and so forth,
> Engagement with the flawless,
> The ripening of beings,
> Cultivation of Buddha-fields,
> Non-abiding transcendence of suffering,
> Supreme enlightenment, and revelation.

To elaborate, these ten are (1) the awakening of the [spiritual] potential and (2) the condition for this awakening, devotion to the Dharma of the Great Vehicle; (3) developing the mind intent on unsurpassable enlightenment and (4) applying oneself to the practice of the six transcendences; (5) reaching the grounds of the noble ones by accessing the flawless on the first Bodhisattva ground; (6) thoroughly ripening beings with skillful means; (7) the purification of Buddha-fields; and (8) the perfection of the qualities of the non-abiding transcendence of suffering through realizing the equality of existence and peace. The last three of these summarize primarily the qualities of the pure grounds. Next, we have (9) the attainment of buddhahood, the final fruition of unsurpassable enlightenment. With this attainment, (10) the genuine revelation of enlightenment continues for as long as existence remains. This revelation entails the uninterrupted [demonstration of] the way of the Buddhas, which is how the form bodies carry out the welfare of sentient beings without interruption for as long as cyclic existence continues.

Just as in that system, in this treatise as well we have (1) the complete presence of the conditions for the awakening of the potential associated with the Great Vehicle, "conditions" here referring to a spiritual master who teaches the Great Vehicle and the rest of the four great wheels.[46] This is the true accomplishment of the potential, the initial cause. (2) Not abandoning the path of the supreme vehicle under any circumstances is the true accomplishment of devotion to the Great Vehicle. (3) Not being distracted by the mental activity characteristic of the Lesser Vehicle is the true accomplishment of the Great Vehicle's mindset. (4) The complete perfection of the six transcendences is the true accomplishment of practice. (5) To give rise to truly transcendent qualities, the path of the noble ones, on the first ground is the true accomplishment of engagement with the flawless. (6) Next, on the [second through] seventh grounds, the fundamental virtues are steadily developed, which is the true accomplishment of the thorough ripening of sentient beings. (7) On the eighth ground, non-conceptual wakefulness makes the mind flexible and a total transformation of the extroverted consciousnesses of the five doors takes place. This is the full accomplishment of the thorough cultivation of Buddha-fields. (8) Through the realization of the equality of existence and peace, the introverted afflicted mental consciousness is transformed. Thus, the nature of the non-abiding transcendence of suffering, which transcends the extremes of cyclic existence and transcendence of suffering, is perceived. This brings about the true accomplishment of prophecy; prophecies are given by the Buddhas regarding one's accomplishment of the irreversible stage. (9) The complete exhaustion of the two obscurations along with their habitual tendencies leads to the absence of obscuration. This is the true accomplishment of supreme enlightenment, the ground of buddhahood. (10) Finally, the uninterrupted manifestation of unsurpassable enlightenment, the nature of the three bodies, is the true accomplishment of the full revelation of enlightenment. This clearly explains the nature of the accomplishments, up to and including the final fruition.

CONCLUSION

The fourth section brings the treatise to a close. This includes (1) a teaching on the difficulty of this treatise and the great qualities it possesses, and (2) the colophons of the author and translators.

THE DIFFICULTY AND GREAT QUALITIES OF THE TREATISE

On the first topic, the treatise states:

> This treatise distinguishes the middle.
> It is hard to comprehend, the essential meaning.
> Deeply meaningful and meaningful for all,
> Everything that is meaningless this dispels. [V.30]

These stanzas on the Unsurpassable Vehicle constitute the fifth chapter of the treatise *Distinguishing the Middle from Extremes.*

Therefore, because it perfectly reveals the path of the Middle Way, **this is a treatise** that **distinguishes the middle.** Since it is inaccessible to logicians, **it is hard to comprehend;** and as it is indestructible in the face of opposition, it is **the essential meaning.** Since it accomplishes the welfare of both oneself and others, it is **deeply meaningful. And,** as it reveals the path of all three vehicles, it is **meaningful for all.** All the afflictive and cognitive obscurations, **everything that is meaningless, this dispels.**

The summary of the Unsurpassable Vehicle has three parts: the practice, the basis for practice, and the result of practice. The practice is presented with the verses that begin: "The topics designated in the Great Vehicle…." That is to say, cultivating calm abiding involves non-distraction, while cultivating insight entails being unmistaken. What is the purpose of these practices? The purpose is to bring about a definitive emergence on the path of the Middle Way. Where does this take place? It takes place on the ten grounds, i.e., that which is known as the specific and the general.

As for being unmistaken, being unmistaken with respect to syllables leads to a full realization of the marks of calm abiding. Being unmistaken about meanings brings full realization of the marks of insight. Being unmistaken about mental activity entirely eliminates the basis of error. Being unmistaken with respect to freedom from conceptual constructs brings an excellent realization concerning the marks of [error]. Being unmistaken with respect to the specific characteristic cultivates the remedy of [error], the non-conceptual path. Being unmistaken about the general characteristic leads to the full realization that it is by nature completely pure. Being unmistaken with respect to purity and impurity brings a full understanding of the elimination and lack of elimination of the obscurations that pertain to the [pure nature]. Being unmistaken with respect to the adventitious occurrence [of impurity and purity] leads to a full realization of thorough affliction and complete purification that accords perfectly with reality. Being unmistaken with respect to fearlessness and absence of conceit allows for the accomplishment of the absence of obscuration, within which there is definitive emergence.

Because it reveals the middle without extremes, the path of the Middle Way, "this treatise distinguishes the middle." In other words, it is a treatise that discerns and distinguishes the middle from the extremes. Because it is extremely profound, logicians will find it hard to comprehend. It is also the essential meaning, that which remains indestructible in the face of opposition, the core meaning of all the vehicles. What it accomplishes is deeply meaningful, insofar as it brings about the temporary and ultimate benefit of both oneself and all others, the unsurpassable fruition. It is also meaningful for anyone with potential for any of the three vehicles. And finally, it dispels the stains of ignorance, misunderstanding, and doubt, as well as the obscurations of affliction and cognition. In other words, it dispels all that is meaningless. As it possesses these five extraordinary qualities, it is indeed a supreme treatise.

This was the commentary to the fifth chapter of the treatise *Distinguishing the Middle from Extremes*, the stanzas on the Unsurpassable Vehicle.

COLOPHONS OF THE AUTHOR
AND THE TRANSLATORS

> This completes the noble Maitreya's composition, *Stanzas on Distinguishing the Middle from Extremes*. The translation was prepared, edited, and established by the Indian preceptors Jinamitra and Śīlendrabodhi together with the great editor of lotsawas, the Bandhe,[47] Zhang Nanam Yeshe De.

> This completes the noble Maitreya's composition, *Stanzas on Distinguishing the Middle from Extremes*. The translation was prepared, edited, and established by the Indian preceptors Jinamitra (i.e., "The Friend of the Victorious One") and Śīlendrabodhi (i.e., "The Master of the Source of Discipline"), together with the great editor of lotsawas, the Bandhe, Zhang Nanam Yeshe De.

The second section concerns the author's colophon, which reads: "This completes the noble Maitreya's composition, *Stanzas on Distinguishing the Middle from Extremes*." The translators' colophon reads: "The translation was prepared, edited, and established by the Indian preceptors Jinamitra and Śīlendrabodhi, together with the great editor of lotsawas, the Bandhe, Yeshe De."

THE COMMENTATORS' COLOPHONS

> These annotations were written by Shenphen Nangwa. They are based on one among the many immaculate works of the emanated lotsawas and paṇḍitas of the past, the commentary of the second Buddha, the master Vasubandhu. May it be virtuous!

From the abyss of inferior views that hold to extremes,
The genuine path of the Middle Way saves us with ease.
This and its gateway for the three types of beings,
Was clearly revealed by the Regent, the supreme Bodhisattva.

The precious treasure of the Buddha's diverse teachings
Is contained herein, this treasury of the vast Dharma.
May these clear and excellent teachings, like a garland of light,
Satisfy all wanderers with the richness of the Dharma.

May all corners of the world be suffused by the light
Of the genuine Dharma through teachings such as this.
May the lotus groves of teaching and practice bloom
And remain as long as existence endures, never withering.

May I as well completely perfect, mature, and cultivate,
Establishing all the infinite forms of sentient life in the supreme
    vehicle.
May the splendor and quality of the Teachings and wandering
    beings flourish.
May all wanderers reach the abode of unexcelled enlightenment.

The exalted life example of Pema Könchog Tenpey Gyaltsan Pal Sangpo,[48] the emanation of Katog Chamla, showed unequalled expertise, purity, and excellence. In raising the victory banner of practice confidently throughout his entire life, he gave perfect joy to the three worlds. Presenting me with an auspicious ceremonial scarf, as well as precious metal of the second order,[49] it was he who first encouraged me to write this commentary. I sincerely kept this master's request in my heart, yet for a while no more became of it.

Later, when I was offering the Dharmas of Maitreya to the precious emanation of Katog Situ,[50] I was provided with conducive circumstances [for writing this commentary], in the form of paper, ink, and other things. Then I, Mipham Nampar Gyalwa, began this composition on the twenty-third day in the month of pūrvabhadrapadā in the year of the wood horse.[51] Continuing to write a bit during the breaks between lectures, I completed this commentary in the early hours of the auspicious fifth day of the following month. It was written at the great seat of Katog

Dorje Den, a place unparalleled in Dokham and renowned as a second Magadha of the Noble Land.

May this fulfill the noble intent of the one who exhorted me to write this and my other masters who have passed on to peace. May it open the eye of the Dharma for future generations and bestow upon all beings, to the farthest reaches of space, the perfect splendor of virtuous goodness, the complete accomplishment of all temporary and ultimate aims.

Sarva Maṅgalam!

Distinguishing the Middle from Extremes

- The meaning of the title
- The translator's homage
- The meaning of the scripture
  - Summary
    - Characteristics
    - Obscurations
    - Reality
    - Cultivation of remedies
    - The bases of this cultivation
    - Attainment of the fruition
    - The Unsurpassable Vehicle
  - Detailed explanation
    - A general perspective on that which is to be understood
      - The objects that are cognized
        - The characteristics of objects of cognition
          - The characteristics of thorough affliction
          - The characteristics of complete purification
        - The obscurations that are eliminated
        - The reality that is realized
      - The path of practice
        - The features of the path
          - The 37 factors of enlightenment and their relationship to the 5 paths
          - A division of these factors into 3 phases
          - The distinguishing features of the Bodhisattva's path
        - The phases of the path
          - 9 phases
          - 3 phases
      - The results of the path
    - The unique approach of the Great Vehicle
      - Brief presentation
      - Detailed presentation
        - Unsurpassable practice
          - The eminent practice
          - The practice of directing the mind
          - The practice of concordant factors
          - The practice of eliminating dualistic extremes
          - The practice of the specific and the general
        - Unsurpassable observation
        - Unsurpassable true accomplishment
- The meaning of the conclusion

APPENDIX

The divisions of emptiness
  The twofold division [I.16]
  The sixteen-part division [I.17-20]
Rationale [I.21]
The obscurations that are eliminated
General presentation [II.1a-c]
Detailed explanation
  The obscurations that prevent liberation
    The actual obscurations [II.1d-2a]
    How they obscure [II.2b-3c]
  The obscurations that inhibit virtue and the rest of the ten qualities
    Brief presentation [II.3d]
    Detailed explanation
      The thirty obscuring factors [II.4-8]
      The ten obscured qualities [II.9]
      An explanation of their relationship [II.10a-b]
    Supplementary explanation: The ten agentive causes [two interspersed stanzas])
  Obscurations that inhibit the three remedies
    Brief presentation [II.10c-d]
    Detailed explanation
      The obscurations associated with the factors of enlightenment [II.11]
      The obscurations associated with the transcendences [II.12-13]
      The obscurations associated with the grounds [II.14-16]
Summary [II.17]
The reality that is realized
Brief presentation [III.1-2]
Detailed explanation
  That which is to be characterized, the reality of the three fundamental and
    essential natures [III.3]
  Explanation of the characteristics of these three [III.4-5b]
  Presentation of the eight principles that relate to them
    Presented in terms of the true meaning [III.5c-8a]
    Presented in terms of cause and effect [III.8b-10a]
    Presented in terms of the subtle and the coarse
      The coarse relative [III.10b-c]
      The subtle ultimate
        The actual ultimate [III.10d]
        Its divisions [III.11]

Presented in terms of the meaning of consensus [III.12a-b]
Presented in terms of what is and is not an object of complete purity [III.12b-c]
Explanation of the summation [III.13]
Explanation of the divisions [III.14]
How they are presented in terms of the ten fields of expertise
    The ten views of self that are eliminated [III.15-16b]
    The ten fields of expertise that eliminate them
        The way in which the ten topics are included in the three natures [III.16c-d]
        How to gain expertise in each of these fields
            Expertise regarding the aggregates [III.17a-b]
            Expertise regarding the elements [III.17c-d]
            Expertise regarding the sense sources [III.18a-b]
            Expertise regarding dependent origination [III.18c-d]
            Expertise regarding the correct and the incorrect [III.19]
            Expertise regarding the faculties [III.20a-b]
            Expertise regarding time [III.20c-d]
            Expertise regarding the truths [III.21]
            Expertise regarding the vehicles [III.22a-c]
            Expertise regarding the conditioned and the unconditioned [III.22d-f]

The path of practice

The features of the path

A presentation of the thirty-seven factors of enlightenment and their
    relationship to the five paths
The four applications of mindfulness that occur on the lesser path of accumulation [IV.1]
The four authentic eliminations that occur on the intermediate path of accumulation [IV.2]
The four bases of miraculous power that occur on the greater path of accumulation
    A brief presentation of the purpose of the four bases of miraculous power
        and the way in which they are produced [IV.3]
    A detailed explanation of their nature
        The five flaws that are eliminated [IV.4]
        How to apply their remedy, the eight applications [IV.5]
The five faculties that occur on the first two stages of the path of joining,
    the stages of heat and summit [IV.6]
The five powers that occur on the last two stages of the path of joining, the
    stages of acceptance and supreme quality [on the path of joining]
    The actual [presentation of the five powers] [IV.7a-b]
    A summation demonstrating how the powers are linked with the path of
        joining [IV.7c-d]

▲▲ ▲

The seven aspects of enlightenment that occur on the path of seeing [IV.8-9b]
The eightfold noble path that occurs on the path of cultivation [IV.9c-11b]
A division of these factors into three phases [IV.11c-12b]
An explanation of the distinguishing features of the Bodhisattva's path [IV.12c-d]
The phases of the path
Nine phases
The actual phases [IV.13]
How they are classified [IV.14-15a]
Three phases [IV.15b-16b]
The results of the path
A general presentation of the five results [IV.16c-17b]
A detailed explanation from the perspective of the path [IV.17c-18]
The unique approach of the Great Vehicle
Brief presentation [V.1a-c]
Detailed explanation
Unsurpassable practice
Brief presentation [V.1d-2c]
Detailed explanation
The eminent practice
The form of practice, the twelve forms of eminence [V.2d-4b]
What is practiced, the ten transcendences
Brief presentation [V.4c-d]
Detailed explanation
The essence of the transcendences [V.5]
Their function [V.6]
The practice of directing the mind
The concise approach: directing the mind using the three types of knowledge
The three types of knowledge [V.7]
Their function [V.8a-b]
The extensive approach: directing the mind via the ten Dharma activities
Brief presentation [V.8c-d]
Detailed explanation
A presentation of the essence and benefits of the ten Dharma
activities [V.9-10b]
An explanation of the unique benefits associated with the
Dharma activities of the Great Vehicle [V.10c-d]
The practice of concordant factors

▼ ▼

Brief presentation [V.11a–b]
Detailed explanation
    Undistracted calm abiding [V.11c–12]
    Unmistaken insight
        Brief presentation [V.13]
        Detailed explanation
            Being unmistaken regarding syllables, the medium for expression [V.14]
            Being unmistaken regarding the meaning they express, which
                is imaginary and lacks any nature [V.15]
            Being unmistaken regarding mental activity, the mere awareness of
                the dependent nature, the cause of dualistic appearances [V.16]
            Being unmistaken by not constructing the two extremes, which occurs
                through realizing dualistic appearance to be illusory and false [V.17]
            Being unmistaken about the thoroughly established nature's specific
                characteristic, its absence of apprehended and apprehender [V.18]
            Being unmistaken about the general characteristic of phenomena,
                knowing that no phenomenon lies outside this non-dual reality [V.19]
            Being unmistaken about the purity and impurity that are based on
                realizing or not realizing reality [V.20]
            Being unmistaken with the knowledge that because the nature [of
                phenomena] is pure, the appearances of purity and impurity
                are adventitious [V.21]
            Being unmistaken regarding the original purity [of all phenomena], which
                ensures that one need not fear being obscured by the thoroughly
                afflictive and being unmistaken in understanding that because [the
                qualities of] complete purification do not develop, there is no [basis for]
                feeling conceited about having such special qualities [V.22]
        Supplementary explanation: A summary, or concise presentation, of the content
            related to the ten ways of being unmistaken that includes a presentation of
            these ten via ten vajra statements [three interspersed stanzas])
The practice of eliminating dualistic extremes
    The first set of seven [V.23–24]
    The second set of seven
        Brief presentation [V.25a–b]
        Detailed explanation [V.25c–26]
The practice of the specific and the general [V.27a–b]
Unsurpassable observation [V.27c–28]

Unsurpassable true accomplishment [V.29]
THE MEANING OF THE CONCLUSION
  A teaching on the difficulty of this treatise and the great qualities it possesses [V.30]
  The colophons of the author and translators

NOTES

1   According to the Tibetan tradition these five are: *Ornament of Manifest Realization* (*Abhisamayālaṃkāra*), *Ornament of the Sutras* (*Sūtrālaṃkāra*), *Distinguishing the Middle from Extremes* (*Madhyāntavibhāga*), *Distinguishing Phenomena from their Intrinsic Nature* (*Dharmadharmatāvibhāga*), and the *Treatise on the Supreme Continuity* (*Uttaratantraśāstra/Ratnagotravibhāga*). In China and Japan the set of five is identified somewhat differently (see MATTHES 1996, 16).

2   See OBERMILLER 2002 and CHATTOPADYĀYA & CHIMPA 1990 for translations of their accounts.

3   *Madhyānatavibhāgabhāsya*. Sanskrit edition in NAGAO 1964. English translation in STANLEY 1988 (including text critical remarks) and ANACKER 1998. English translation of chapter I in KOCHUMUTTOM 1982. WOOD 1991 contains a translation of the root verses of chapter I. Japanese translation is provided in NAGAO 1976.

4   *Madhyāntavibhāgaṭīkā*. YAMAGUCHI 1966 provides a Sanskrit edition based on an incomplete manuscript and the Tibetan translation (YE SHES SDE c). STANLEY 1988 contains an English translation accompanied by text critical remarks. English translation of chapter I in STCHERBATSKY 1992 and FRIEDMANN 1937.

5   For a survey and discussion of differing accounts, both ancient and modern, of the authorship of the Maitreya treatises and the identity of Vasubandhu, see MATTHES 1996.

6   YE SHES SDE a.

7   YE SHES SDE b (English translation of chapter I in STCHERBATSKY 1992 and of chapter III in O'BRIEN 1953) and YE SHES SDE c.

8   For a biography of Khenpo Shenga, see NYOSHUL KHENPO 2005. THONDUP 1999, JACKSON 2004, and DREYFUS (forthcoming) likewise contain many

valuable biographical details. An account of Shenga's life prepared by Adam Pearcy is available online (www.lotsawahouse.org).

9   GZHAN DGA' 1999.

10   The thirteen classics encompass two texts on vinaya (the *Prātimokṣasūtra* and Guṇaprabhā's *Vinayasūtra*), two treatises on abhidharma (*Abhidharmakośa* by Vasubandhu and *Abhidharmasamuccaya* by Asaṅga), four works on madhyamaka (*Mūlamadhyamakakārikā* by Nāgārjuna, *Madhyamakāvatāra* by Candrakīrti, *Catuḥśataka* by Āryadeva, and *Bodhicaryāvatāra* by Śāntideva) and the five treatises by Maitreya.

11   On Shenga's role in the Rimé movement and his commentaries to the thirteen classics see note 8.

12   For a biography, see PETTIT 1999. Two of the works most central to Mipham's philosophical approach, the *Beacon of Certainty* (*Nges shes sgron me*) and his commentary on the *Ornament of the Middle Way* (*Madhyamakālaṃkāra*), are available in English translation (the former in PETTIT 1999 and the latter in MIPHAM 2004a and SHANTARAKSHITA & MIPHAM 2005). Mipham's renowned guide to Buddhist philosophy, the *Gateway to Knowledge (mKhas pa'i tshul la 'jug pa'i sgo)*, presents an extremely detailed commentary to *Distinguishing the Middle from Extremes*, chapter III, stanzas 15-23 (English translation in MIPHAM 1997-2002). Mipham's commentary to another of Maitreya's five treatises, the *Dharmadharmatāvibhāga*, is translated into English in MIPHAM 2004b and into German in MATTHES 1996. Mipham's philosophical approach has recently been studied in PETTIT 1999, PHUNTSHO 2005, and DUCKWORTH 2005.

13   MI PHAM 1990.

14   To help the reader maintain an overview of this quite complex, multilayered structure, the text of the outline has been separately compiled in an appendix to the translations.

15   For the sake of clarity we have constructed headings to the various sections of the text. Note that while the headings are based on Mipham's topical outline they occasionally differ substantially from the actual text of the outline. In the appendix, all titles are extracted from the text of the outline.

16   Cf. MI PHAM 2004a, 457-59, 683.

17   Note that the asterisk therefore simply indicates that a given Sanskrit word cannot be found in Vasubandhu's commentary. Contrary to the common academic practice, it does not necessarily imply that the given word is a doubtful reconstruction.

18 This has been done despite the fact that on a few occasions the Sanskrit differs from the Tibetan in the way that it separates root-text from Vasubandhu's commentary. Where such discrepancy occurs it has been noted it in the footnotes.

19 In Tibet discussions have centered on the related issues of whether the philosophical approach of the text should be seen as Mind Only (*sems tsam*) or Middle Way (*dbu ma*), and whether its teaching is of 'expedient' (*drang don, neyārtha*) or 'definitive meaning' (*nges don, nītārtha*). See for example MIPHAM 2004b, 59-63 and MATTHES 1996, 15-17, 181-85.

20 "The Kinsman of the Sun" is an epithet for Buddha Śākyamuni.

21 Maitreya.

22 Tib. *dBus dang mtha' rnam par 'byed pa tshig le'ur byas pa.*

23 Tib. *dbus mtha'.*

24 Both here and in the Sanskrit title to Mipham's commentary, the text in fact reads *vibhega*. We have sought to correct this and other apparent printing errors in the title. The full Sanskrit title to Mipham's commentary actually reads: *Rasmimālanāmamadhyantavibhegasyśastaṃsya ṭīka viharati sma.*

25 Tib. *nam par 'byed pa.*

26 Tib. *le'ur 'byed pa.*

27 If one doesn't affirm the conventional existence of the false imagination and doesn't negate the existence of the apprehended and apprehender (which is the same as affirming emptiness), the absurd consequence of accepting the opposite will follow; one will be denying the conventional existence of the false imagination while affirming the existence of the apprehended and apprehender.

28 The essence of consciousness refers to the primary mind.

29 Tib. *tshur rol mthong ba.* This term literally means "seeing this side," referring to the limited perception of those in cyclic existence as opposed to the vision of the Noble Ones.

30 In Nagao's Sanskrit edition, the last two lines are part of Vasubandhu's prose, not the original text (see NAGAO 1964).

31 The following section contains sets of three obscurations, each of which applies to one of the ten qualities, making thirty obscurations in total.

32 The level of inspired conduct refers to the path of accumulation and the path of joining.

33   Tib. *don spyi.* Object universals are the constructed objects that the conceptual mind relates to.

34   The term for "sense source" in Tibetan is *skye mched,* the individual syllables of which literally mean "arising" and "spreading."

35   I.e. the mind mistakenly believes that the constructed concept of the absence self in fact captures reality.

36   In Nagao's Sanskrit edition, this line is part of Vasubandhu's prose, not the original text (see NAGAO 1964).

37   These eight are the states of hell beings, starving spirits, animals, long living gods, barbarians, beings with wrong view, beings with impaired mental faculties, and those born in a place where the Dharma is not present. In these eight states one is not free to practice the Dharma.

38   In Nagao's Sanskrit edition, this line is part of Vasubandhu's prose, not the original text (see NAGAO 1964).

39   Here the specific and the general practice are counted as one, making five topics rather than six.

40   The original discussion is in terms of Tibetan rather than English.

41   The following twelve verse lines were entered into the root text by the master Vasubandhu as an explanation of the ten ways of being unmistaken. Drawing from the sūtras of the Great Vehicle, Vasubandhu presents the ten in the form of "vajra statements" (*vajrapadā, rdo rje tshig*). The sequence of the ten vajra statements follows that of the ten ways of being unmistaken, which they explain.

42   The vajra statements are presented individually in the following section.

43   The translation of points 8-10 follows Vasubandhu's commentary. The editions of Shenphen Nangwa's commentary that were available to us here read: "(8) full realization; (9) the total expansion entailed in achieving the path of seeing; (10) the understanding up to the seventh ground."

44   The three spheres are those of object, agent, and action.

45   These four are discrimination regarding the Dharma, meanings, definitive words, and eloquent courage

46   These four are living in a conducive place, serving holy beings, making aspirations, and gathering merit.

47   *Bandhe* is the Sanskrit term for a Buddhist monk.

48   Born in the nineteenth century, Pema Könchog Tenpey Gyaltsan Pal Sangpo (*kaḥ tog pa lcam la sprul pa'i sku padma dkon mchog bstan pa'i rgyal mtshan dpal bzang po*) was a regent of Katog Dorje Den (*kaḥ tog rdo rje ldan*), one of the six main monastic centers of the Nyingma school of Buddhism in Tibet. This master is also known as Chamtrul Könchog Chöphel (*lcam sprul dkon mchog chos 'phel*).

49   "Precious metal of the second order" is a poetic term for silver.

50   Katog Situ Chökyi Gyatso (*kaḥ tog si tu chos kyi rgya mtsho*), 1880-1923/25.

51   1894.

52   The titles that appear in the appendix have been extracted from the actual text of Mipham's outline. These titles therefore at times differ substantially from the constructed subheads that have been entered into the translation (see n. 15).

ENGLISH - TIBETAN
GLOSSARY

A

absence of self	bdag med
absorption	ting nge 'dzin
acceptance	bzod pa
access	'jug pa
accomplishment	'grub pa
accumulation	tshogs
adventitious	lo bur ba
affliction	nyon mongs
afflictive obscuration	nyon sgrib
afflictive thorough affliction	nyon mongs pa'i kun nas nyon mong pa
agentive cause	byed rgyu
aggregate	phung po
agility	shin tu sbyang ba
agitation	rgod pa
alertness	shes bzhin
all-ground	kun gzhi
appearance	snang ba
application of mindfulness	dran pa nye bar bzhag pa
apprehend	'dzin pa, gzung ba
apprehended	gzung ba
apprehender	'dzin pa
appropriation	nyer len
argument	gtan tshig
aspect	cha, yan lag
aspect of enlightenment	byang chub kyi yan lag
aspect of the noble path	'phags lam yan lag

aspiration	smon lam
attachment	chags pa
authentic	yang dag pa
authentic elimination	yang dag par spong ba
awareness	rnam rig

B

base of miraculous power	rdzu 'phrul gyi rkang pa
basic field of phenomena	chos kyi dbyings
basis	gnas, gzhi
becoming	srid pa
belief	lta ba
bewilderment	rmongs pa
Bodhisattva	byang chub sems dpa'
body of perfect enjoyment	long spyod rdzogs pa'i sku
body of qualities	chos kyi sku
bond	kun sbyor
brightness	dwang ba
Buddha	sangs rgyas

C

calm abiding	zhi gnas
categories, five	dngos po lnga
categorization	rnam grangs
category	rnam grangs
causal thorough affliction	rgyu'i kun nas nyon mongs pa
cessation	'gog pa
characteristic	mtshan nyid
classification	rnam grangs, rnam gzhag
coarse	rags pa
coemergent	lhan skyes
cognitive obscuration	shes sgrib
collection of consciousness	rnam par shes pa'i tshogs
concentration	bsam gtan
concept	rtog pa
concordant factor	mthun phyogs
conditioned	'dus byed
conducive	cha dang mthun pa
conducive factor	mthun phyogs

consciousness	rnam par shes pa
consensus	grags pa
contact	reg pa
convention	tha snyad
correct discrimination	so sor yang dag par rig pa
craving	sred pa
cultivation	sgom pa
cyclic existence	'khor ba

D

dedication	sngo ba
defiled mental cognition	nyon mongs pa'i yid
defiling	zags bcas
definitive emergence	nges par 'byung ba
denial	skur 'debs
denigration	skur 'debs
dependent [nature]	gzhan dbang
dependent origination	rten 'brel
depreciation	skur 'debs
determination	yongs su gcod pa
development of the enlightened mind	sems bskyed
devotion	mos pa
Dharma	chos
Dharma activity	chos spyod
diligence	brtson 'grus
directing the mind	yid la byed pa
discard	spang bya
discipline	tshul khrims
discordant factor	mi mthun phyogs
disenchantment	skyo ba
distinction	khyad par
division	dbye ba
doubt	the tshom
dullness	bying ba

E

effect	'bras bu
effect of individual effort	skyes bu byed pa'i 'bras bu
effect of separation	bral ba'i 'bras bu

effect that accords with the cause	rgyu mthun gyi 'bras bu
element	khams
eliminated factor	spang bya
eliminated through cultivation	sgom spang
elimination	spong ba
emanation body	sprul pa'i sku
eminent	dam pa
emptiness	stong pa nyid
engage	'jug pa
enlightened mind	byang chub kyi sems
enlightenment	byang chub
enlightenment, aspect of	byang chub kyi yan lag
entity	dngos po
equality	mnyam pa nyid
equanimity	btang snyom
equilibrium	snyoms 'jug
equipoise	mnyam gzhag
error	phyin ci log pa
essence	ngo bo
essential nature	ngo bo nyid
established	grub pa
exaggeration	sgro btags
existence	yod pa, srid pa
experience	nye bar spyod pa, snang ba
expert	mkhas pa
external object	phyi don
extreme	mtha'

F

factor of enlightenment	byang chub kyi phyogs kyi chos
faculty	dbang po
faith	dad pa
false imagination	yang dag par ma yin pa'i kun rtog
feasible	'thad pa
field	spyod yul, zhing
field of expertise	mkhas bya'i gnas
flaw	nyes pa
flexible	las su rung ba
focus	dmigs pa

form	gzugs
formation	'du byed
foundation	gzhi
freedom from conceptual constructs	spros bral, mi 'phro ba
fruition	'bras bu
fundamental transformation	gnas yongs su gyur ba

G

generosity	sbyin pa
genuine	yang dag pa
grasping	len pa
Great Vehicle	theg pa chen po
ground	gzhi, sa
ground of inspired conduct	mos spyod kyi sa

H

habitual tendency	bag chags
heat	dro ba
hostility	sdang ba

I

identification	'du shes
identity	bdag nyid
ignorance	ma rig pa
imaginary [nature]	kun brtags
imagination	kun rtog
imputed	kun btags, kun brtags
inference	rjes dpag
innate	lhan skyes
insight	lhag mthong
inspiration	mos pa
instruction	gdams ngag
intellectual	rtog ge
intent	bsam pa
intention	'dun pa
interest	mos pa
intrinsic nature	chos nyid

K

karma	las
karmic thorough affliction	las kyi kun nas nyon mongs pa
knowledge	shes rab

L

latency	bag nyal
Lesser Vehicle	theg pa dman pa
liberation	thar pa
life-force faculty	srog dbang
linguistic symbol	brda
Listener	nyan thos
livelihood	'tsho ba
logician	rtog ge
luminous	'od gsal ba

M

manifest	mngon gyur
mark	mtshan ma
mastery	dbang ba
material needs	yo byad
meaning	don
means	thabs
meditation	sgom pa
meditative absorption	ting nge 'dzin
meditative equipoise	mnyam gzhag
mental activity	yid la byed pa
mental state	sems byung
method	thabs
Middle Way	dbu ma
mind	blo, sems
mind generation	sems bskyed
mind of enlightenment	byang chub kyi sems
mindfulness	dran pa
mind stream	rgyud
mistaken	phyin ci log pa
mistaken view	log lta
mundane	jig rten pa

N

name and form	ming gzugs
nature	don, rang bzhin
negandum	dgag bya
negative tendency	gnas ngan len
noble	'phags pa
non-conceptuality	rnam par mi rtog pa
non-conceptual wakefulness	rnam par mi rtog pa'i ye shes
non-entity	dngos med
non-existence	med pa

O

object	don, yul
object of cognition	shes bya
object universal	don spyi
obscuration	sgrib pa
observation	dmigs pa
observation of perfect purity	rnam par dag pa'i dmigs pa
origin	kun 'byung
origination	kun 'byung

P

partake of	nye bar spyod pa
path	lam
path beyond training	mi slob lam
path of accumulation	tshogs lam
path of cultivation	bsgom lam
path of joining	sbyor lam
path of seeing	mthong lam
patience	bzod pa
perception, direct	mngon sum
perfectly genuine	yang dag pa'i mtha'
perpetuation	nyer len
phenomenon	chos
pleasurable states	bde 'gro
potential [spiritual]	rigs
power	stobs
practice	sgrub pa, 'jug pa
predominant effect	bdag po'i 'bras bu

pride	nga rgyal
primary mind	gtso sems
principle	rnam grangs, rnam gzhag
proclamations in song	dbyangs kyis bsnyad pa
property	chos
property possessor	chos can
purification, complete	rnam byang
purity	dag pa
pursuit	ched du bya ba

Q
quality	chos, yon tan

R
rational	'thad pa
real	bden pa, yang dag pa
reality	de kho na nyid, don
realization	rtogs pa
realm	khams, gnas
reasonable	'thad pa
re-existence	yang srid
relative	kun rdzob
relinquishment	spong ba
remedy	gnyen po
result	'bras bu
resultant thorough affliction	'bras bu'i kun nas nyon mongs pa
ripened effect	rnam smin gyi 'bras bu
ripening	rnam smin

S
sacred	dam pa
sameness	mnyam pa nyid
self	bdag
selflessness	bdag med
Self-realized Buddha	rang sangs rgyas
sense source	skye mched
sentient being	sems can
significance	don
sphere [of engagement]	spyod yul

spiritual practice	rnal 'byor
stain	dri ma
stainless	dri med
stream of being	rgyud
study	thos pa
subject	chos can, yul can
subsequent attainment	rjes thob
subsidiary affliction	nye ba'i nyon mong pa
substance	rdzas
subtle	phra ba
subtle developer	phra rgyas
suchness	de bzhin nyid
summit	rtse mo
superimposition	sgro btags
superior	khyad par du 'phags pa
super-knowledge	mngon shes
supramundane	'jig rten las 'das pa
supreme property	chos mchog
Sutra of the Definitive Explanation of the Intent	mdo dgongs pa nges par 'grel pa
Sutra on Numerous Elements	khams mang po can gyi mdo
synonym	rnam grangs

T

tenet	grub mtha'
thesis	dam bca'
thorough affliction of birth	skye ba'i kun nas nyon mongs pa
thoroughly established [nature]	yongs grub
thought	rtog pa
train	sgom pa, slob pa
transcendence	'das pa, pha rol du phyin pa
true	bden pa, yang dag pa

U

ultimate	don dam
unconditioned	'dus ma byed
universal emperor	'khor los sgyur ba
universally present meaning	kun tu 'gro ba'i don
unmistaken	phyin ci ma log pa

V

validation	tshad ma
vessel	gnod
view	lta ba
view of the transitory collection	'jig tshogs lta ba
virtue	dge ba
volition	sems pa

W

wakefulness	ye shes
world	'jig rten
world of sentient beings	bcud kyi 'jig rten
world of the receptacle	gnod kyi 'jig rten

TIBETAN - ENGLISH - SANSKRIT GLOSSARY *

KA

Tibetan	English	Sanskrit
kun tu 'gro ba'i don	the universally present meaning	sarvatragārtha
kun btags	imputed	*parikalpita
kun rtog	imagination	parikalpa
kun brtags	the imaginary [nature], imputed	parikalpita
kun 'byung	origin, origination	samudaya
kun sbyor	bond	saṃyojana
kun rdzob	relative	saṃvṛti
kun gzhi	all-ground	ālaya
skur 'debs	denigration, depreciation	apavāda
skye mched	sense source	āyatana
skye ba'i kun nas nyon mongs pa	thorough affliction of birth	janma-saṃkleśa
skyes bu byed pa'i 'bras bu	result of individual effort	puruṣakāra-phala
skyo ba	disenchantment	udvega, parikheda

KHA

Tibetan	English	Sanskrit
khams	element, realm	dhātu
khams mang po can gyi mdo	*Sutra on Numerous Elements*	Bahudhātuka-sūtra
khyad par	distinction, particularity	viśeṣa

---

* In this glossary, an asterisk simply indicates that a given Sanskrit word cannot be found in the Sanskrit edition of Vasubandhu's commentary. Contrary to the common academic practice, it does not necessarily imply that the given word is a doubtful reconstruction.

khyad par du 'phags pa	distinct, superior	viśiṣṭa, vaiśeṣika
mkhas pa	expertise, expert	kauśalya, paṇḍita
mkhas bya'i gnas	field of expertise	
'khor ba	cyclic existence	saṃsāra
'khor los sgyur ba	universal emperor	cakra-vartin

GA

grags pa	consensus	prasiddha(ka)
grub mtha	tenet	siddhānta
dgag bya	negandum	*pratiṣedhya
dge ba	virtue	kuśala, śubha
'gog pa	cessation	nirodha
'grub pa	accomplishment, establishment	niṣpatti, prasiddha, siddhi
rgod pa	agitation	uddhata, auddhatya
rgyu mthun gyi 'bras bu	effect that accords with the cause	niṣyanda-phala
rgyu'i kun nas nyon mongs pa	causal thorough affliction	hetu-saṃkleśa
rgyud	[mind-]stream, stream of being	santāna
sgom pa	cultivation, meditation, training	bhāvanā
sgrib pa	obscuration	āvaraṇa, āvṛti, chādana, nivaraṇa
sgrub pa	practice	pratipatti, prapatti, prapannatā, sādhana
sgro btags	exaggeration, superimposition	āropa, samāropa
bsgom spang	eliminated through cultivation	bhāvanāheya
bsgom lam	path of cultivation	bhāvanā-mārga

NGA

nga rgyal	pride	abhimāna, unnati, māna
nges par 'byung ba	definitive emergente	niryāṇa
nges 'byed cha mthun	factor that accords with ascertainment	nirvedha-bhāgīya
ngo bo	essence	svabhāva
ngo bo nyid	essential nature	svabhāva, svābhāvikatva
dngos po	entity	bhāva, vastu
dngos po lnga	five categories	pañca vastūni
dngos med	non-entity	abhāva
mngon gyur	manifest	*abhimukhi
mngon shes	super-knowledge	abhijñā
mngon sum	direct perception	pratyakṣa
sngo ba	dedication	nati

CHA

cha dang mthun pa	conducive factor	bhāgīya
chags pa	attachment	sakti
ched du bya ba	pursuit	adhikāra
chos	dharma, phenomenon, property, quality	dharma
chos kyi sku	body of qualities	dharmakāya
chos kyi dbyings	basic field of phenomena	dharmadhātu
chos can	property possessor, subject	*dharmin
chos mchog	supreme property	agra-dharma
chos nyid	intrinsic nature	dharmatā

chos spyod bcu	ten Dharma activities	daśadhā-dharma-carita

JA

'jig rten	world	loka
'jig rten pa	of the world, mundane,	laukika
'jig rten las 'das pa	beyond the world, supramundane	lokottara
'jig tshogs la lta ba	view of the transitory collection	satkāya-dṛṣṭi
'jug pa	access, engage, practice	avakrānti, avatṛ-, praviś-, praveśa, pravṛt-, viśāra, sāra
rjes thob	subsequent attainment	*pṛṣṭhalabdhajñāna
rjes dpag	inference	*anumāna

NYA

nyan thos	Listener	śrāvaka
nye ba'i nyon mongs pa	subsidiary affliction	upakleśa
nye bar spyod pa	experience, encounter	upabhoga
nyer len	appropriation, perpetuation	upādāna
nyes pa	flaw	doṣa
nyon sgrib	afflictive obscuration	kleśāvaraṇa
nyon mongs pa	affliction	kleśa
nyon mongs pa'i kun nas nyon mong pa	afflictive thorough affliction	kleśa-saṃkleśa
nyon mongs pa'i yid	defiled mental cognition	kliṣṭaḥ manaḥ
gnyen po	remedy	pratipakṣa, vipakṣa
mnyam pa nyid	equality, sameness	samatā

Tibetan	English	Sanskrit
mnyam gzhag	[meditative] equipoise	*samādhā,
snyoms 'jug	equilibrium	samāpatti

TA

Tibetan	English	Sanskrit
ting nge 'dzin	absorption, meditative absorption	samādhi
gtan tshig	argument	hetu
btang snyoms	equanimity	upekṣā, samupekṣā
rten 'brel	dependent origination	pratītya-samutpāda
rtog ge	intellectual, logician	tārkika
rtog pa	concept, thought	kalpanā
rtogs pa	realization	adhigama, anubudhyana, anubodha, praveśa
lta ba	belief, view	darśana, dṛṣṭi
stong pa nyid	emptiness	śūnyatā
stobs	power	bala

THA

Tibetan	English	Sanskrit
tha snyad	convention	*vyavahāra
thabs	means, method	upāya
thar pa	liberation	mokṣa
the tshom	doubt	vicikitsā
theg pa chen po	the Great Vehicle	mahāyāna
theg pa dman pa	the Lesser Vehicle	hīnayāna
thos pa	study	śruta
mtha'	extreme	anta

mthun phyogs	concordant factor, conducive factor	*sapakṣa
mthong lam	path of seeing	darśana-mārga
'thad pa	feasible, reasonable, sound	*upapatti

DA

dag pa	purity	śuddhi
dad pa	faith	śraddhā
dam bca'	thesis	pratijñā
dam pa	eminent, sacred	parama
de kho na nyid	reality	tattva
de bzhin nyid	suchness	tathatā
don	object, meaning, nature, reality, significance	artha, bhāva
don dam	ultimate	paramārtha
dran pa	mindfulness	smṛti
dran pa nye bar bzhag pa	application of mindfulness	smṛty-upasthāna
dri ma	stain	mala
dri med	stainless	amala, nirmala
dro ba	heat	uṣma
gdams ngag	instruction	avavāda
bdag	self	ātman
bdag nyid	identity	ātman
bdag po'i 'bras bu	predominant effect	adhipati-phala
bdag med	absence of self, selflessness	nairātmya

Tibetan	English	Sanskrit
bde ' gro	pleasurable states	sugati
bden pa	real, true	sat
mdo dgongs pa nges par 'grel pa	Sutra of the Definitive Explanation of the Intent	Saṃdhinirmocanasūtra
'du byed	formation	saṃskāra
'dun pa	intention	chanda
'dus byed	conditioned	saṃskṛta
'dus ma byed	unconditioned	asaṃskṛta
'du shes	identification	saṃjñā
brda	linguistic symbol	*saṃketa

NA

Tibetan	English	Sanskrit
gnas	basis, realm, state	adhiṣṭhāna, avasthā, āśraya, pratiṣṭhā, sanniśraya, sthāna, sthiti
gnas ngan len	negative tendency	dauṣṭhulya
gnas yongs su gyur ba	fundamental transformation	*āśrayaparāvṛtti
rnam grangs	categorization, classification, principle, synonym	paryāya
rnam rtog	concept, thought	vikalpa
rnam par dag pa	purity	viśuddhi
rnam par dag pa'i dmigs pa	observation of perfect purity	viśuddhy-ālambana
rnam par mi rtog pa	non-conceptuality	avikalpana, nirvikalpa
rnam par mi rtog pa'i ye shes	non-conceptual wakefulness	avikalpana jñāna, nirvikalpa jñāna
snam par smin pa'i 'bras bu	ripened effect	vipāka-phala

rnam par shes pa	consciousness	vijñāna
rnam par shes pa'i tshogs	collection of consciousness	vijñāna-kāya
rnam byang	complete purification	vyavadāna
rnam smin	ripening	vipāka
rnam gzhag	category, classification, principle	vyavasthāna, vyavasthāpana
rnam rig	awareness	vijñapti
rnal 'byor	spiritual practice	yoga
snang ba	appearance, experience	darśana, prakhyāna, pratibhās-, pratibhāsa
gnod	vessel	bhājana
gnod kyi 'jig rten	world vessel	bhājanaloka

PA

spang bya	discarded factor, eliminated factor	prahātavya, heya
spong ba	elimination, relinquishment	tyāga, prahāṇa, vivarjana
spyod yul	field, sphere [of engagement]	gocara
sprul pa'i sku	emanation body	nirmāṇa-kāya
spros bral	freedom from conceptual constructs	*nisprapañca

PHA

pha rol du phyin pa	transcendence	pāramitā
phung po	aggregate	skandha
phyi don	external object	bāhyārtha
phyin ci ma log pa	unmistaken	aviparīta, aviparyasta
phyin ci log pa	error, mistaken	viparyasta, viparyāsa

phra rgyas	subtle developer	*anuśaya
phra ba	subtle	sūkṣma
'phags pa	noble	ārya
'phags lam yan lag	aspect of the noble path	ārya-mārga-aṅga

BA

bag chags	habitual tendency	vāsanā
bag nyal	latency	*anuśaya
byang chub	enlightenment	bodhi
byang chub kyi phyogs	factor of enlightenment	bodhipakṣya
byang chub kyi yan lag	aspect of enlightenment	bodhyaṅga
byang chub kyi sems	enlightened mind, the mind of enlightenment	bodhicitta
byang chub sems dpa'	Bodhisattva	bodhisattva
bying ba	dullness	laya
byed rgyu	agentive cause	karaṇa
bral ba'i 'bras bu	effect of separation	visaṃyoga-phala
dbang po	faculty	indriya
dbang ba	mastery	vaśitā
dbu ma'i lam	path of the Middle Way	madhyamā pratipat
dbyangs kyis bsnyad pa	the proclamations in song	geya
dbye ba	division	bheda
sbyin pa	generosity	dāna
sbyor lam	path of joining	prayoga-mārga

Tibetan	English	Sanskrit
'bras bu	fruition, result	phala
'bras bu'i kun nas nyon mongs pa	resultant thorough affliction	phala-kleśa

MA

Tibetan	English	Sanskrit
ma rig pa	ignorance	avidyā
mi mthun phyogs	conflicting factor, discordant factor	vipakṣa
mi 'phro ba	freedom from conceptual constructs	aviśāra
mi slob lam	path beyond training	aśaikṣa-mārga
ming gi rnam grangs	synonym	paryāya
ming gzugs	name and form	nāma-rūpa
med pa	non-existence	abhāva, asat, asattva
mos pa	devotion, inspiration, interest	adhimukti, adhimokṣa
mos spyod kyi sa	ground of inspired conduct	adhimukticaryā-bhūmi
dmigs pa	focus, observation	ālambana, upalabdhi, upalambha
rmongs pa	bewilderment	moha, vimoha, saṃmoha
smon lam	aspiration	praṇidhāna

TSA

Tibetan	English	Sanskrit
rtse mo	summit	mūrdhāna
gtso sems	primary mind	*citta
brtson 'grus	diligence	vīrya

TSHA

Tibetan	English	Sanskrit
tshad ma	validation	pramāṇa

Tibetan	English	Sanskrit
tshul khrims	discipline	śīla
tshogs	accumulation	kāya, sambhāra
tshogs lam	path of accumulation	sambhāra-mārga
mtshan nyid	characteristic	lakṣaṇa
mtshan ma	mark	nimitta
mtshan ma med pa	absence of marks	ānimittā, nimittābhāva, nirnimittatā
'tsho ba	livelihood	ājīva

DZA

Tibetan	English	Sanskrit
'dzin pa	apprehend, apprehender	grahaṇa, grāha, grāhaka
rdzas	substance	*dravya, *upadhi
rdzu 'phrul gyi rkang pa	base of miraculous power	ṛddhipāda

ZHA

Tibetan	English	Sanskrit
zhi gnas	calm abiding	śamatha
gzhan dbang	dependent [nature]	paratantra
gzhi	basis, ground, foundation	ādhāra, nidhāna, vastu

ZA

Tibetan	English	Sanskrit
zags bcas	defiling	sāsrava
gzugs	form	rūpa
gzung ba	apprehended	grāhya
bzod pa	acceptance, patience	kṣānti

'A

Tibetan	English	Sanskrit
'od gsal ba	luminous	prabhāsvara

YA

Tibetan	English	Sanskrit
yang dag pa ji lta bzhin	in perfect accordance with reality	yathābhūta
yang dag pa	authentic, genuine, real, true	bhūta
yang dag mtha'	the perfectly genuine	bhūtakoṭi
yang dag par 'grub pa	true accomplishment	samudāgama
yang dag par spong ba	authentic elimination	samyakprahāṇa
yang dag par ma yin pa'i kun rtog	false imagination	abhūta-parikalpa
yang srid	re-existence	punar-bhava
yan lag	aspect	aṅga
yid la byed pa	directing the mind, mental activity	manaskāraṇa, manasikāra, manasikriyā, manaskāra
yul	object	viṣaya
yul can	subject	*viṣayin
ye shes	wakefulness	jñāna
yo byad	material needs	pariṣkāra
yo byad bsnyungs	few material needs	saṃlekha
yongs grub	thoroughly established [nature]	pariniṣpatti, parinispanna
yongs su gcod pa	determination	pariccheda
yod pa	existence	astitva, bhāva, sadbhāva
yon tan	good quality, quality	guṇa
g.yeng ba	distraction	vikṣepa

RA

rags pa	coarse	udāra, audārika
rang bzhin	nature	prakṛti, svabhāva
rang sangs rgyas	Self-realized Buddha	pratyekabuddha
rigs	[spiritual] potential	gotra
reg pa	contact	sparśa

LA

lam	path	pratipad, pratipatti, mārga
las	karma	karman
las kyi kun nar nyon mongs pa	karmic thorough affliction	karma-saṃkleśa
las kyi mtha'	activity	karmānta
las su rung ba	flexible	karmaṇya
len pa	grasping	upādāna
lo bur ba	adventitious	āgantuka
log lta	mistaken view	mithyā-dṛṣṭi
long spyod rdzogs pa'i sku	body of perfect enjoyment	sāmbhogikaḥ kāyaḥ

SHA

shin tu sbyangs ba	agility	praśrabdhi
shes sgrib	cognitive obscuration	jñeyāvaraṇa
shes bya	object of cognition	jñeya
shes bzhin	alertness	samprajanya
shes rab	knowledge	prajñā

SA

sa	ground	bhūmi
sangs rgyas	Buddha	buddha
sems	mind	citta, cetas
sems bskyed	development of the enlightened mind	cittotpāda
sems can	sentient being	sattva
sems pa	volition	cintana, cetana
sems byung	mental state	caitta
so sor yang dag par rig pa	correct discrimination	pratisaṃvid
srid pa	existence, becoming	bhava, sambhava
sred pa	craving	tṛṣṇā
srog dbang	life-force faculty	jīvitendriya
slob pa	someone training	śaikṣa
bsam gtan	concentration	dhyāna
bsam pa	intent, reflection	abhisandhi, āśaya

HA

lhag mthong	insight	vipaśyanā
lhan skyes	coemergent, innate	sahaja

BIBLIOGRAPHY

ANACKER, STEFAN. 1998. *Seven Works of Vasubandhu: The Buddhist Psychological Doctor.* Delhi: Motilal Banarsidass.

CHATTOPADHYĀYA, ALAKA & LAMA CHIMPA. 1990. *Tāranātha's History of Buddhism in India.* Delhi: Motilal Banarsidass.

DUCKWORTH, DOUGLAS S. 2005. "Buddha-Nature and a Dialectic of Presence and Absence in the Works of Mi-pham." PhD diss., University of Virginia.

DREYFUS, GEORGES. Forthcoming. "Where Do Commentarial Schools Come From? Reflections on the History of Tibetan Scholasticism." *Journal of the International Association of Tibetan Studies.* www.jiats.org.

FRIEDMANN, DAVID L. 1937. *Sthiramati: Madhyāntavibhāgaṭīkā: Analysis of the Middle Path and the Extremes.* Utrecht: Utrecht University.

NĀGĀRJUNA. 1986. *Mūlamadhyamakakārikā: The Philosophy of the Middle Way.* Trans. David J. Kalupahana. Albany: State University of New York Press.

GZHAN DGA'. 1999. *dBus dang mtha' rnam par 'byed pa'i mchan 'grel.* Ed. TARTHANG TULKU RINPOCHE. Berkeley: Yeshe De Project.

JACKSON, DAVID P. 2004. *A Saint in Seattle: The Life of the Tibetan Mystic Dezhung Rinpoche.* Boston: Wisdom Publications.

KOCHUMUTTOM, THOMAS A. 1982. *A Buddhist Doctrine of Experience.* Delhi: Motilal Banarsidass.

MATTHES, KLAUS-DIETER. 1996. *Unterscheidung der Gegebenheiten von ihrem wahren Wesen (Dharmadharmatavibhāga): Eine Lehrschrift der Yogācāra-Schule in tibetischer Überlieferung.* Swisttal-Odendorf: Indica et Tibetica Verlag.

MIPHAM, JAMGON JU. 1990. *dBus dang mtha' rnam par 'byed pa'i bstan bcos kyi 'grel ba 'od zer phreng ba.* In *Sde-dge dgon-chen Prints of the Writings of 'Jam-mgon 'Ju Mi-pham-rgya-mtsho.* Ed. DILGO KHYENTSE. Vol. 4, 659-785. Kathmandu: Shechen Monastery.

———. 1997-2002. *Gateway to Knowledge: A Condensation of the Tripitaka.* 3 vols. Trans. Erik Pema Kunsang. Boston: Rangjung Yeshe Publications.

———. 2004a. *Speech of Delight: Mipham's Commentary on Śāntarakṣita's* Ornament of the Middle Way. Trans. Thomas H. Doctor. Ithaca, N.Y.: Snow Lion Publications.

———. 2004b. *Maitreya's Distinguishing Phenomena and Pure Being with Commentary by Mipham.* Trans. Jim Scott. Ithaca, N.Y.: Snow Lion Publications.

NAGAO, GADJIN. 1964. *Madhyāntavibhāga-bhāṣya.* Tokyo: Suzuki Research Foundation.

———. 1976. *Daijō Butten.* Vol. 15, 215-358, 380-409.

NYOSHUL, KHENPO JAMYANG DORJE. 2005. *A Marvelous Garland of Rare Gems: Biographies of Maters of Awareness in the Dzogchen Lineage (A Spiritual History of the Teachings of Natural Great Perfection).* Junction City: Padma Publishing.

O'BRIEN, P.W. 1953. "A Chapter on Reality from the Madhyāntavibhāgaśāstra." In *Monumenta Japonica,* vol. 9, 277-303.

OBERMILLER, EUGENE. 2002 (first edition 1932). Trans. *The History of Buddhism in India and Tibet by Bu-ston.* Delhi: Paljor Publications.

PEARCY, ADAM. 2006. "Biography of Khenpo Shenga (1871-1927)." www.lotsawahouse.org.

PETTIT, JOHN WHITNEY. 1999. *Mipham's* Beacon of Certainty: *Illuminating the View of Dzogchen, the Great Perfection.* Boston: Wisdom Publications.

PHUNTSHO, KARMA. 2005. *Mipham's Dialectics and the Debates on Emptiness: To Be, Not To Be Or Neither.* London: RoutledgeCurzon.

SHANTARAKSHITA & JAMGON MIPHAM. 2005. *The Adornment of the Middle Way: Shantarakshita's* Madhyamakalankara *with Commentary by Jamgon Mipham.* Trans. Padmakara Translation Group. Boston: Shambhala.

STANLEY, RICHARD. 1988. "A Study of the Madhyāntavibhāga-bhāṣya-ṭīka." PhD diss. Australian National University, Canberra, Australia.

STCHERBATSKY, THEODORE. 1992 (first edition 1936). *Madhyāntavibhanga: Part 1 Translated from Sanskrit*. Delhi: Sri Satguru.

THONDUP, TULKU. 1999. *Masters of Meditation and Miracles: Lives of the Great Buddhist Masters of India and Tibet*. Boston: Shambhala.

YAMAGUCHI, SUSUMU. 1966. *Sthiramati: Madhyāntavibhāgaṭīka*. Tokyo: Suzuki Research Foundation.

YE SHES SDE (a). Trans. *dBus dang mtha' rnam par 'byed pa'i tshig le'ur byed pa*. 4021 in the sDe dge edition of the Tibetan Tripiṭaka.

———. (b). Trans. *dBus dang mtha' rnam par 'byed pa'i 'grel pa*. 4027 in the sDe dge edition of the Tibetan Tripiṭaka.

———. (c). Trans. *dBus dang mtha' rnam par 'byed pa'i 'grel bzhad*. 4032 in the sDe dge edition of the Tibetan Tripiṭaka.

WOOD, THOMAS. 1991. *Mind Only: A Philosophical and Doctrinal Analysis of the Vijñānavāda*. Honolulu: University of Hawaii Press.

INDEX